INTRODUCING
ISSUES WITH
OPPOSING
VIEWPOINTS®

UFOs

UFOs

Other books in the Introducing Issues
with Opposing Viewpoints series:

INTRODUCING
ISSUES WITH
OPPOSING
VIEWPOINTS®

UFOs

Jamuna Carroll, *Book Editor*

Bonnie Szumski, *Publisher*
Helen Cothran, *Managing Editor*
Lauri S. Friedman, *Series Editor*

GREENHAVEN PRESS
An imprint of Thomson Gale, a part of The Thomson Corporation

THOMSON
™
GALE

Detroit • New York • San Francisco • San Diego • New Haven, Conn. • Waterville, Maine • London • Munich

For more information, contact
Greenhaven Press
27500 Drake Rd.
Farmington Hills, MI 48331-3535
Or you can visit our Internet site at http://www.gale.com

LIBRARY OF CONGRESS CATALOGING-IN-PUBLICATION DATA

UFOs / Jamuna Carroll, book editor.
    p. cm. — (Introducing issues with opposing viewpoints)
  Includes bibliographical references and index.
  ISBN 0-7377-3227-X (lib. : alk. paper)
  1. Unidentified flying objects. I. Carroll, Jamuna. II. Series.
  TL789.U218 2006
  001.942—dc22

                                               2005055147

Contents

Foreword

I ndulging in a wide spectrum of ideas, beliefs, and perspectives is a critical cornerstone of democracy. After all, it is often debates over differences of opinion, such as whether to legalize abortion, how to treat prisoners, or when to enact the death penalty, that shape our society and drive it forward. Such diversity of thought is frequently regarded as the hallmark of a healthy and civilized culture. As the Reverend Clifford Schutjer of the First Congregational Church in Mansfield, Ohio, declared in a 2001 sermon, "Surrounding oneself with only like-minded people, restricting what we listen to or read only to what we find agreeable is irresponsible. Refusing to entertain doubts once we make up our minds is a subtle but deadly form of arrogance." With this advice in mind, Introducing Issues with Opposing Viewpoints books aim to open readers' minds to the critically divergent views that comprise our world's most important debates.

Introducing Issues with Opposing Viewpoints simplifies for students the enormous and often overwhelming mass of material now available via print and electronic media. Collected in every volume is an array of opinions that captures the essence of a particular controversy or topic. Introducing Issues with Opposing Viewpoints books embody the spirit of nineteenth-century journalist Charles A. Dana's axiom: "Fight for your opinions, but do not believe that they contain the whole truth, or the only truth." Absorbing such contrasting opinions teaches students to analyze the strength of an argument and compare it to its opposition. From this process readers can inform and strengthen their own opinions, or be exposed to new information that will change their minds. Introducing Issues with Opposing Viewpoints is a mosaic of different voices. The authors are statesmen, pundits, academics, journalists, corporations, and ordinary people who have felt compelled to share their experiences and ideas in a public forum. Their words have been collected from newspapers, journals, books, speeches, interviews, and the Internet, the fastest growing body of opinionated material in the world.

Introducing Issues with Opposing Viewpoints shares many of the well-known features of its critically acclaimed parent series, Opposing Viewpoints. The articles are presented in a pro/con format, allowing readers to absorb divergent perspectives side by side. Active reading questions preface each viewpoint, requiring the student to approach the material thoughtfully and carefully. Useful charts, graphs, and cartoons supplement each article. A thorough introduction provides readers with crucial background on an issue. An annotated bibliography points the reader toward articles, books, and Web sites that contain additional information on the topic. An appendix of organizations to contact contains a wide variety of charities, nonprofit organizations, political groups, and private enterprises that each hold a position on the issue at hand. Finally, a comprehensive index allows readers to locate content quickly and efficiently.

Introducing Issues with Opposing Viewpoints is also significantly different from Opposing Viewpoints. As the series title implies, its presentation will help introduce students to the concept of opposing viewpoints, and learn to use this material to aid in critical writing and debate. The series' four-color, accessible format makes the books attractive and inviting to readers of all levels. In addition, each viewpoint has been carefully edited to maximize a reader's understanding of the content. Short but thorough viewpoints capture the essence of an argument. A substantial, thought-provoking essay question placed at the end of each viewpoint asks the student to further investigate the issues raised in the viewpoint, compare and contrast two authors' arguments, or consider how one might go about forming an opinion on the topic at hand. Each viewpoint contains sidebars that include at-a-glance information and handy statistics.

Following in the tradition of the Opposing Viewpoints series, Greenhaven Press continues to provide readers with invaluable exposure to the controversial issues that shape our world. As John Stuart Mill once wrote: "The only way in which a human being can make some approach to knowing the whole of a subject is by hearing what can be said about it by persons of every variety of opinion and studying all modes in which it can be looked at by every character of mind. No wise man ever acquired his wisdom in any mode but this." It is to this principle that Introducing Issues with Opposing Viewpoints books are dedicated.

Introduction

"There could hardly be any discovery more dramatic or important than visitors from other worlds."

—Seth Shostak, SETI (Search for Extraterrestrial Intelligence) Institute

One weekend in 1947 a mysterious object crashed on Mack Brazel's ranch near Roswell, New Mexico. Pieces of shiny, remarkably durable, and extremely lightweight material were strewn across the ground. Oddly, Brazel's sheep would not venture across the debris. Moreover, the material reportedly had strange hieroglyphic-type writing on it. Immediately upon learning of the wreckage, the Roswell Army Air Field dispatched two senior officers who gathered the debris. Although the military initially said it had recovered a flying disk, it soon retracted that statement and explained the object had been a weather balloon. But, Brazel told the *Roswell Daily Record* at the time, "I am sure what I found was not any weather observation balloon."[1] Because of the government's hastiness to send military to the location and its changing story about the crash, rumors began to swirl about what happened in Roswell. Some locals speculated that evidence of an alien spacecraft had been concealed. To this day, what happened at Roswell remains fodder for countless television shows, movies, writings, and discussion among curious people all over the world.

Alleged UFO encounters such as the one at Roswell are fascinating because they call into question whether humans are alone in the universe. For centuries humans have speculated about the existence of advanced extraterrestrial (ET) life, yet have uncovered no hard proof of it. Around the time of the Roswell incident, scientists began to comb the skies for evidence. It was thought that radio or optical signals might be discovered, indicating the existence of other civilizations in the universe.

The search for extraterrestrial intelligence (sometimes abbreviated as SETI) often focuses on narrowband radio signals, such as radar and satellite. Scientists believe these types of signals would not occur naturally in the universe and so their presence would indicate intelligent activity. The giant radio telescope at the Arecibo Observatory in Puerto Rico surveys the sky for such signals. Analyzing the data that is continuously produced by the telescope requires a lot of computing power, though. Therefore, the telescope is linked to a unique program called SETI@home that allows nearly anyone to use their home computer to aid in the search. Internet users can download a screen saver program that takes advantage of their computer's unused processing cycles. When users leave their computers on and idling, the program automatically downloads data collected by the telescope, analyzes the data for unique patterns that might represent an intelligent transmission, and sends it back to the research team. Signals with a high likelihood of originating from an intelligent civilization are observed again

This illustration depicts a UFO struck by lightning over Roswell, New Mexico, on July 2, 1947. In the inset photo, military officials examine fragments recovered from the Roswell crash site.

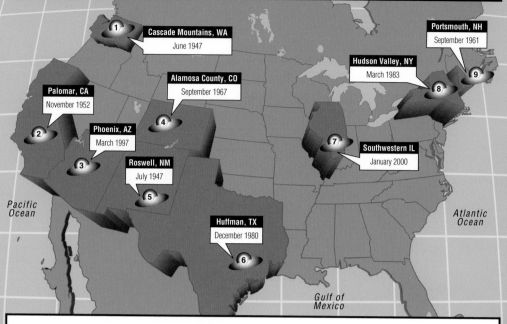

Well-Known Extraterrestrial Sightings in the United States

Cascade Mountains, WA
June 1947

Portsmouth, NH
September 1961

Hudson Valley, NY
March 1983

Alamosa County, CO
September 1967

Palomar, CA
November 1952

Phoenix, AZ
March 1997

Roswell, NM
July 1947

Southwestern IL
January 2000

Huffman, TX
December 1980

Pacific Ocean

Atlantic Ocean

Gulf of Mexico

1. Pilot Kenneth Arnold reports "flying saucers."
2. George Adamski claims to meet an ET and travel with it.
3. Thousands of citizens observe a V-shaped formation of lights moving over the city.
4. ETs are blamed for deaths of farm animals.
5. UFO debris is discovered; alleged government cover-up ensues.
6. Betty Cash and Vickie and Colby Landrum experience adverse reactions after coming in contact with a UFO.
7. Police officers track a UFO across several towns.
8. A huge triangular aircraft is spotted by hundreds of people.
9. Barney and Betty Hill claim to be abducted by aliens.

later. So far over 2 million people worldwide use SETI@home and 5 billion potential signals have been logged.

Another project that will search for the radio waves of alien civilizations is California's Allen Telescope Array (ATA), currently under construction by the SETI Institute and the University of California at Berkeley. As one of the largest and most powerful telescopes in the world, it will consist of 350 19.7-foot (6m) dishes that can survey a million or more stars while amplifying signals from the sky. The telescope's advantage over previous systems is that it is more sensitive, has less interference, and is capable of examining several stars simultaneously, rather than one star at a time, for twenty-four hours a day. The SETI Institute predicts, "For the first time in its forty-year history, SETI [Institute] will be able to check out a truly significant sample of the cosmic haystack.

The enormous radio telescope at the Arecibo Observatory in Puerto Rico is designed to search the sky for signals from extraterrestrial civilizations. Pictured is the telescope's receiver.

This is not an incremental step forward: the Allen Telescope Array will increase the stellar reconnaissance by orders of magnitude."[2]

Instead of searching for radio signals of intelligent civilizations, some scientists look for bright light pulses or laser beacons that they believe would better indicate the presence of an intelligent civilization. Stuart A. Kingsley of the Columbus Optical SETI Observatory notes, "For the past quarter of a century, popular books and articles about SETI have said little if anything about the benefits of lasers for free-space interstellar communications."[3] Those who agree that ETs would be more likely to use light than radio to communicate with other life-forms tend to support optical searches like the one under way at the University of California's Lick Observatory. Using a 40-inch (101.6 cm) telescope in conjunction with a new pulse-detection system, researchers there hope to detect powerful, fast-flashing beacons from light-years away. Frank Drake of the SETI Institute maintains, "This is perhaps the most sensitive optical SETI search yet undertaken."[4]

Despite their efforts, scientists have not uncovered any evidence of intelligent ET life thus far. Nor have they found concrete proof that UFOs are alien spaceships. Some do not believe that such evidence will ever be found. Astronomer Guillermo Gonzalez explains, "While I was a 'believer' in ETI [extraterrestrial intelligence] most of my life, I changed my mind about 10 years ago, after I thought carefully about the astronomical and geophysical requirements for advanced life in the universe."[5] He and astronomer Hugh Ross conclude, "The universe appears to be finely tuned for humans."[6] However, other undiscouraged researchers point out that the world and the universe are so vast it will just take much time before we stumble across signs of ETs or their spaceships.

As exemplified by the continued search for ET signals and by the enduring stories behind alleged UFO encounters, many people remain captivated by the possibility of aliens visiting Earth. The search for proof of ETs and their spacecraft thus continues. Both skeptics and believers have produced a fascinating array of explanations for the mysterious objects seen soaring above Earth. A compendium of such theories—both earthly and extraterrestrial—is presented in *Introducing Issues with Opposing Viewpoints: UFOs.*

Notes

1. *Roswell Daily Record,* "Harassed Rancher Who Located 'Saucer' Sorry He Told About It," July 9, 1947.
2. SETI Institute, "Allen Telescope Array General Overview," www.seti.org, 2005.
3. Stuart A. Kingsley, "Introduction to the COSETI Web Site," The Columbus Optical SETI Observatory, October 15, 2000. www.coseti.org.
4. Space.com, "SETI to Search for Extraterrestrial Laser Light," www.space.com, July 24, 2001.
5. Guillermo Gonzalez, "Alien Intelligence? Think Again," www.space.com, February 29, 2000.
6. Guillermo Gonzalez and Hugh Ross, "Home Alone in the Universe," *First Things,* May 2000.

Chapter 1

What Are UFOs?

A computer-generated image depicts alien spaceships just outside the Earth's atmosphere.

UFOs Are Alien Spaceships

Dennis Balthaser

"There is proof that extraterrestrial craft with intelligent occupants have visited our planet."

In the following selection Dennis Balthaser presents evidence that many UFOs are extraterrestrial spacecraft. He discusses physical marks left at the sites of UFO landings and videotapes of UFOs in the sky. He believes the large number of unexplained sightings and abductions that have been reported by witnesses is additional proof that aliens are visiting this planet. Balthaser is a UFOlogist who is involved with HBCC UFO and Skywatch International, organizations that investigate UFO sightings.

AS YOU READ, CONSIDER THE FOLLOWING QUESTIONS:
1. Why are most UFO sightings never reported, in the author's opinion?
2. What two examples show that UFOs have existed for thousands of years, according to Balthaser?
3. How does the author define "proof"?

UFOs (Unidentified Flying Objects) are not debatable; they're *a fact of life*. What UFOs are, some think is debatable. I suppose that's where the disagreement starts. We have an enormous amount of physical evidence, and I do not understand why [skeptics] won't accept the proof that has already been produced. Perhaps if we had a piece of metal or other material from an actual craft, some would tend to agree that we have been, and are being, visited by extraterrestrials from another world. Many of us believe that our government does in fact have such physical proof, but we have not yet been able to obtain it. The government may have good reason to withhold the proof, but I can't speak for them. I will try in this editorial to explain some of what we do have as physical evidence and proof.

Numerous UFO Encounters

Several well-documented cases come to mind. The 1964 Socorro, New Mexico, Lonnie Zamora case had imprints in the soil from a craft, as well as burnt vegetation around the area. Within hours, an Army Intelligence agent from White Sands [New Mexico], as well as an FBI agent investigated it. When [the Air Force's] Project Blue Book ended their study of UFOs in 1969, this case was still listed as unknown. A

"I'm getting tired of being mistaken for a weather balloon!"

In April 1964 researchers in Socorro, New Mexico, search for evidence of a UFO landing after local police officer Lonnie Zamora (inset) reported an extraterrestrial sighting.

U.S. Military Base in England had the same thing, as well as an "audio recording" of the event. The [1967] Shag Harbor [Nova Scotia] case reportedly produced a green film on the water. [A UFO over] Maury Island [Washington] had its "debris" analyzed in Chicago and Washington State, not to mention what the military investigated. The 1947 Roswell [New Mexico] Incident, had material scattered over a large area of the impact site, recovered by the military, and it has never been seen again. And there are more cases.

Our judicial system in the United States is set up where one eyewitness' testimony is enough to find a defendant guilty, and sentence that person to life imprisonment or even execution. There is no physical proof involved there either. Many of the witnesses that have come forward over the years pertaining to UFOs are very distinguished, professional, respectable individuals, but the critics won't believe them, even though some of those names included the biggest names in the military as well as the intelligence community. Consequently, to avoid embarrassment or ridicule, most sightings or experiences with UFOs are never reported. For our politicians, apparently admitting to knowledge about UFOs would be politically devastating. Perhaps that's why many of our leaders are not informed about the UFO situation. Who has given certain individuals the authority to withhold information?

Documentation of Flying Saucers

I have in previous editorials mentioned some phrases in the Bible that many believe are UFO related; the ancient artwork from the 1300 and 1400's that show what appear to be UFOs in these artwork masterpieces; and other examples of UFO existence for thousands of years. We cannot, nor should we, ignore that, simply because we are not displaying a piece of a crashed craft or a recovered alien as physical proof. It's now believed that the Egyptian pyramids are thousands of years older than we've originally been told, and in the future I hope to research the possibility of alien involvement in the building of the pyramids, if in fact they were built in pre-Egyptian time.

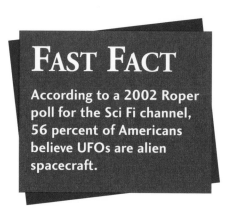

FAST FACT

According to a 2002 Roper poll for the Sci Fi channel, 56 percent of Americans believe UFOs are alien spacecraft.

With the use of video cameras in recent years, many sightings have been recorded by thousands of individuals and the images on those films cannot be explained satisfactorily. Examples include hundreds of people video taping the [mile-long, triangular-shaped] Phoenix Lights [in 1997], the Mexico sightings from all over that country, taken simultaneously and reported by every major media outlet in Mexico (but not here in the states). In the U.S. there are thousands of hours of videotape of UFOs, many authenticated by "experts", both government and civilian. The same holds true for photographs. Granted, some are hoaxes or explainable, but not all and it's time we were told about them.

Regardless of what the Air Force says about not being interested in UFOs or not investigating them, we now have enough documentation through the efforts of reliable historical Ufologists to prove that the United States Air Force has investigated UFOs and still is, regardless of what their Public Relations personnel say. Forensic experts have authenticated some of these documents, which indicate a possible conspiracy by certain individuals within our government to keep this quiet. We have in our possession military and governmental documents to support our proof. In addition, the government has admitted to lying about UFOs on several occasions on the subject of UFOs. Look up the CIA, NSA, and FBI on your computer and see what they are saying on this subject, and while doing that, think about what they are not telling you.

There Is Proof of UFOs

The *Random House Dictionary of the English Language* states as the first definition of the word "Proof"— *"evidence sufficient to establish a thing as true, or to produce belief in its truth"*. I firmly believe we have met those criteria.

Some of the people that claim to have been abducted by extraterrestrials have unexplainable marks on their bodies, implants, missing time in their lives, etc. Radar screens have detected objects that are unexplainable, based on their speed and movement, when no aircraft

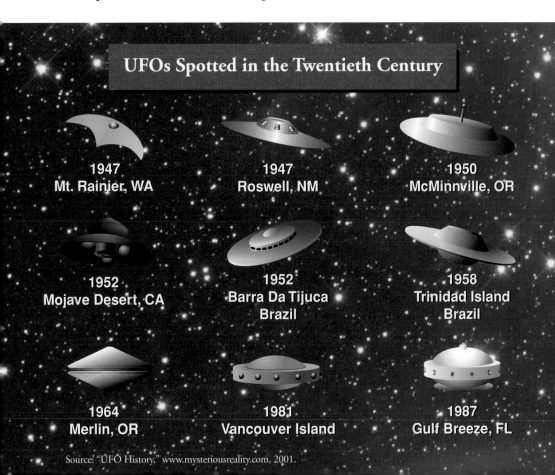

UFOs Spotted in the Twentieth Century

| 1947 | 1947 | 1950 |
| Mt. Rainier, WA | Roswell, NM | McMinnville, OR |

| 1952 | 1952 | 1958 |
| Mojave Desert, CA | Barra Da Tijuca Brazil | Trinidad Island Brazil |

| 1964 | 1981 | 1987 |
| Merlin, OR | Vancouver Island | Gulf Breeze, FL |

Source: "UFO History," www.mysteriousreality.com, 2001.

This intricate crop-circle design appeared in a California wheat field in 2003. Some people believe crop circles are created by alien spacecraft.

are reported in the area of the radar units at the time of the observation. Our own and other countries' military aircraft have scrambled to chase after UFOs, only to find they cannot catch them or they completely disappear from the pilots' view. All of these examples are well documented, yet we are asked, "where's the proof"?

Most People Are Unaware of the Evidence

In my opinion, many of those that want proof, really don't want it, because once they are given that proof, they manage to distort the facts and truth to continue their own agenda as is the case with several researchers/authors on the subject of Ufology. Also, certain members of the military and our government have had years of practice in denying any involvement with UFOs. In their case, I believe we are now accumulating enough documentation to prove that they are interested and are involved, and sooner or later will have to admit to the public that there is proof that extraterrestrial craft with intelligent occupants have visited our planet.

Researcher Stanton Friedman addressed this subject of proof or evidence some time ago and has graciously agreed to let me quote what he said about it.

The case for the flying saucer reality is far better than the case against most convicted criminals. If you do it on an evidential basis, you can look at things like [UFO researcher] Ted Phillips' collected information on over 5,000 physical trace cases from 70 countries. These are cases where the saucer is seen on or near the ground, and after it leaves, one finds clear physical changes such as burn circles and burn rings, landing gear marks, swirled vegetation, dried out soil, and so forth. People say there is no physical evidence. Well, if a footprint and a fingerprint are physical evidence, then the physical trace cases are certainly physical evidence. In addition, the same things keep happening all over the world. The problem is most people are unaware of the evidence, even though there is a preponderance of evidence. Given the physical trace cases, the radar sightings, the photographs and the eyewitness testimony from people all over the world, we have quite sufficient evidence to conclude that our planet is being visited by manufactured objects behaving in ways that we Earthlings cannot yet duplicate, and that therefore were produced someplace else.

EVALUATING THE AUTHOR'S ARGUMENTS:

The author compares the UFO phenomenon to the U.S. court system, concluding that neither requires physical proof to make decisions. Is hard evidence necessary to prove the existence of alien craft, in your opinion? Why or why not?

UFOs Are Military Aircraft

Steve Douglass

"Unidentified 'airships' have been spotted by airline pilots and civilians who report them as UFOs."

People who think they have seen alien spaceships have actually caught a glimpse of top-secret military spy ships, suggests Steve Douglass in the following viewpoint. Douglass, the editor of Utility Communications Digest in *Popular Communications Magazine,* attributes several famous UFO sightings to manmade craft. He writes that spy ships usually prowl high in the skies to collect sensitive information for the government. But sometimes they are forced down into lower airspace where they can be spotted by cilivians. He reasons that the proximity of UFO sightings to restricted military ranges means that the ships do in fact belong to the military.

AS YOU READ, CONSIDER THE FOLLOWING QUESTIONS:
1. What did the pilot of the American Air West 727 think he saw, according to the author?
2. What are the government's stealth ships capable of doing, in the author's opinion?
3. According to Douglass, what was the proposed design of the Lockheed HI-SPOT?

Steve Douglass, "Are UFOs in Actuality the Military's Ultimate Sky Spies?" *Popular Communications Magazine,* August 2004. Copyright © 2004 by Steve Douglass. Reproduced by permission.

If the winds were kind and the technical problems were ironed-out, by the time you read this you may have already heard about the strange "flying V-shaped" UFO that has been seen by citizens over far west Texas and southeastern New Mexico.

Although the event hasn't happened as of this writing [in mid-2004], it is likely this huge flying object will be seen at sunset and is flying so high it probably glows bright for maybe more than an hour after dusk and will undoubtedly prompt uninformed citizens to call local authorities and report an unidentified flying object in the area.

An Amazing Spy Ship

In reality the UFO is a prototype of a new lighter-than-air sky spy and might give utility monitors in the area a rare opportunity to intercept some unique communications.

Scheduled for late June [2004] and lasting throughout the summer and fall, a V-shaped airship bigger than a baseball diamond is due to rise from the West Texas desert to an altitude of 100,000 feet (30.5 km), navigate by remote control, linger above the clouds and drift back to earth.

UFO sightings may actually be attributed to sophisticated military spy ships, such as the Nighthawk stealth fighter pictured here.

This joint JP Aerospace/U.S. Air Force project to build a new kind of reconnaissance and battlefield communications platform some day might lead to even bigger lighter-than-air, gas filled floating platforms that gossamer spaceships could use as high-altitude way stations.

"The full-size station in our grand vision is 2 miles across," says John Powell, the company's founder. "But that's down the road a bit. We take baby steps." . . .

Known as the "Ascender" the unique shaped aerostat is slated to be (as of press-time) launched from the Pecos County/West Texas Spaceport at Fort Stockton, TX, but the liftoff is dependent on the weather and has been delayed several times. . . .

Why Stealth Ships Are Thought to Be UFOs

Although the Ascender is considered to be a prototype of a future system, there are some who speculate the NRO [National Reconnaissance Office] has been flying top-secret airships for years which have been responsible for many "slow moving" UFO sightings.

This photo captures a band of hazy red and white lights suspended over a town in England.

A few years ago an American Air West 727 was flying in an air corridor just north of the restricted military airspace known as Area 51, when lightning from a nearby thunderstorm illuminated a huge motionless cigar-shaped object hovering silently over the Nevada Desert. The pilot, startled by the sudden appearance of the eerie craft, radioed air traffic controllers to report the encounter as a UFO sighting.

Controllers on the ground responded that it was probably a classified aircraft operating out of the restricted Nellis Range. The pilot described the craft as looking something like an elongated big black blimp, invisible except when illuminated by lightning flashes.

What the commercial pilot saw was most likely one of the best kept black world secrets, the

stealth airship, a flying Big Brother, prowling the upper reaches of the atmosphere capable of collecting enormous amounts of intelligence for its spy masters on the ground.

These rumored "stealth-ships" are capable of eavesdropping on military, government and civilian radio communications, photographing the world below in amazing detail, and even listen with sensitive electronic ears for the telltale sounds of war.

Possibly equipped with state of the art imaging devices, ground scanning radars and sonic detection equipment, unmanned sky spies could go completely unnoticed until something goes wrong.

They are only spotted when, as fate would have it, a kink in the jet stream forces these goliaths down into civil airspace where they can become a hazard to commercial aircraft traffic and visible to us groundlings below. On many occasions unidentified "airships" have been spotted by airline pilots and civilians who report them as UFOs.

Could it be that the famous Belgian, Mexico City and Hudson Valley UFO sightings of a huge, slow moving aircraft, accompanied by large formations of military helicopters, are in reality stealth-ships accidentally brought down to low altitude by freakish winds?

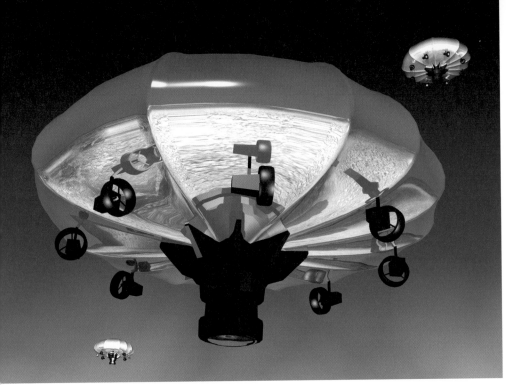

This computerized look at the underside of a high-altitude stealth airship shows how the craft might resemble a flying saucer to a casual observer on the ground.

Although eye-witness reports by qualified observers point to the possible existence of stealth air ships, new documentation almost goes as far as proving it.

The Evidence Points to Secret Military Ships

Lockheed-Martin (the same company that designed the SR-71 Blackbird and F-117 stealth fighter) recently secured patents on advanced airship designs with the U.S. Patent Office.

The concept for a high altitude reconnaissance airship is not new and has its roots in the U.S. Navy's HI-SPOT program of the late 1970s. HI-SPOT (High Surveillance Platform for Over-the Horizon Targeting) addressed the Navy's stated needs for a lighter-than air reconnaissance platform. . . .

In 1981, the NADC (Naval Air Development Center) selected the Lockheed Missiles and Space Company to develop HI-SPOT. According to information Lockheed released to the press in that same year, the Lockheed HI-SPOT design would be that of an unmanned blimp-like airship 500 feet long.

Shortly after the press release the HI-SPOT program was classified as top secret with no announcements ever coming from the Pentagon that the system was cancelled or fielded; however multiple sightings of slow-moving rigid airships reported by many observers in Nevada and California began surfacing in the mid to late 1980s.

In 1990, a major sighting of a slow-moving black airship occurred in California's Antelope Valley not very far from one of Lockheed's secret radar cross section testing ranges. The airship was described as being 500 to 600 feet long, blotting out the night sky while moving slower than four miles per hour. Artist depictions of a huge pumpkin seed shaped airship were published in *Aviation Week Magazine* (10-1-90) and other aviation technology publications.

Such a huge airship would need to be based in huge hangars. Just such a large hangar has been photographed at the secret Area 51 base in Nevada.

Recently this author also spotted very large hangars capable of housing airships on the Fort Bliss Range. . . . These hangars may account for the 1995 sighting of a large black airship by an airline crew flying near Las Cruces, New Mexico. Las Cruces sits on the west side of the Ft. Bliss Range.

EVALUATING THE AUTHOR'S ARGUMENTS:

Douglass argues that UFOs are manmade spy ships that citizens do not yet know about. Some UFO believers, on the other hand, maintain that only some UFO sightings are governmental aircraft and the rest involve alien spaceships. Which conclusion is more plausible, in your opinion? Why?

UFOs Are Celestial Bodies

Ian Ridpath

"Astronomical objects are by far the main causes of mistaken UFO reports."

Celestial bodies such as stars, planets, and meteors are the main sources of UFO reports, claims Ian Ridpath in the following viewpoint. The natural characteristics of celestial bodies combined with faulty human perception makes them easily mistakable for UFOs, Ridpath declares. For example, he writes, viewers often misjudge the distance, size, and brightness of astronomical bodies. Even objects as familiar as the moon can sometimes be mistaken for flying saucers, he says. Ridpath is a UFO skeptic who has written and edited several astronomy handbooks, including the *Princeton Field Guide to Stars and Planets.*

AS YOU READ, CONSIDER THE FOLLOWING QUESTIONS:
1. Name six celestial bodies Ridpath believes are commonly mistaken as UFOs.
2. What does the author call the biggest UFO culprit of all?
3. How does Ridpath explain the report in which three witnesses saw a hovering saucer with two pulsating lights?

A mateur astronomers know more about the causes of UFO sightings than most so-called UFO researchers. [Science fiction writer] Arthur C. Clarke, not a man with a closed mind, once said: "If you've never seen a UFO, you're not very observant. And if you've seen as many as I have, you won't believe in them."

To see what he meant, we need to look at some statistics. Astronomical objects are by far the main causes of mistaken UFO reports. In a classic analysis of 1,300 UFO reports made to the Center for UFO Studies in the US, published by Allan Hendry in *The UFO Handbook*, just over half of all identified nocturnal lights were accounted for by astronomical causes: stars, planets, meteors, the Moon, artificial satellites, and satellite re-entries.

What's more, astronomical objects also featured prominently among the identified daytime UFOs, those involving apparent corroboration by radar, and the various classes of close encounters, including the celebrated Third Kind in which occupants are supposedly sighted. In short, an astronomical solution should always be uppermost in a UFO investigator's mind, but experience shows that few UFOlogists have even a rudimentary understanding of astronomy and so fail to weed out even easily explicable cases.

Characteristics of Celestial Bodies

Why should simple lights in the sky cause such confusion? As amateur astronomers know, most people are totally unfamiliar with the sky. Highly credible witnesses such as teachers, policemen and pilots (yes, and astronomers) can still be surprised by the unexpected appearance of a bright star, planet, meteor, or satellite.

Usually, a description such as "it seemed to hover for an hour" is diagnostic of a star or planet (people get fed up watching after about an hour, or the object sets). Often there are other descriptions such as "flashing coloured lights" or "it appeared to be rotating" which are good descriptions of the way stars appear to behave, notably Sirius on a cold, frosty night. Binoculars do not always help identification if they happen to be cheap and with optical defects that produce spurious colours and shapes.

Additional information such as "it wasn't there before" or "it appeared to move slowly" or "it dodged around" are still consistent with characteristics of stars and planets. Many people don't realize that stars rise

This large cloud seen at sunset from atop Mauna Kea on the island of Hawaii looks uncannily like a flying saucer.

and set during the night. Thin clouds can make stars appear to dim and brighten, as though they were receding or approaching. And, when seen between scudding clouds, stars really do appear to dodge around.

Errors in Perception

A more subtle effect is known technically as the autokinetic effect. In this, natural movements of the eye make a stationary object appear to move irregularly, sometimes zooming up and down or swinging from side to side in a movement sometimes described as like a "falling leaf." Autokinetic motion can be uncanny when watching artificial satellites, which often appear to zig zag or even make deviations around stars in their path.

Another shortcoming of human perception is that it is impossible to judge the distances of lights in the sky. A planet millions of miles away, an aircraft several thousand feet away, or a torch bulb a few dozen yards away all appear much the same size and brightness at night. The examples in this article show the tendency of witnesses to grossly underestimate the distance of nocturnal lights.

Venus

Let's start by looking at some instructive examples involving the planet Venus, the biggest UFO culprit of all, popularly known as the "evening star" (although it can also appear in the morning sky as the "morning star"). As amateur astronomers know, Venus is the brightest object in the night sky after the Moon and can dazzle the eye, sometimes appearing cross-shaped. Back in 1967, there was a famous case in which two policemen in Devon, England, reported Venus as a UFO shaped like a "flying cross" and chased it in their car at speeds up to 90 mile/h.

Perhaps the most celebrated UFO witness of all time was the governor of the US state of Georgia, a former American naval officer trained in celestial navigation and nuclear physics, who was later to become president of the United States: Jimmy Carter. In 1973, Carter reported that four years earlier he and 10 other people in the town of Leary, Georgia, had watched a brilliant UFO low on the horizon which appeared to move towards them and away again, while changing in

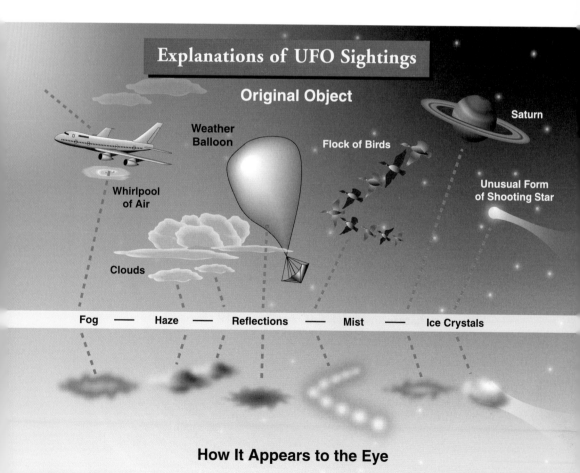

Explanations of UFO Sightings

Original Object

Weather Balloon

Flock of Birds

Saturn

Unusual Form of Shooting Star

Whirlpool of Air

Clouds

Fog — Haze — Reflections — Mist — Ice Crystals

How It Appears to the Eye

brightness, size, and colour. He estimated the distance as between 300 ft and 1,000 ft, and said that at times it became almost as big and bright as the full Moon.

This case was thoroughly investigated by Robert Sheaffer, who described it in his book *The UFO Verdict*. For a start, Sheaffer found that Carter was nine months out in his recollection of the date. Of the ten claimed witnesses, Sheaffer could find only one who remembered the incident even vaguely, and he thought the object might have been a balloon. But with the correct date established, Sheaffer found that the witnesses had been looking straight at brilliant Venus. The errors in his report are typical of those made by UFO witnesses: the size and brightness of the object is overestimated, the distance is underestimated, and spurious motion is attributed to the object. . . .

Explaining a Classic UFO Case

It is understandable that people can misidentify planets and bright stars—but surely not the Moon? Yet it happens. Allan Hendry describes a case in which three witnesses observed a saucer "25 ft in diameter" accompanied by two pulsating lights which hovered over a car park for nearly an hour, dimming the car park lights as though draining power from them. A humming noise was heard which changed to a loud beeping before the saucer shot straight up into the sky. A parakeet owned by one of the witnesses screeched and her dogs barked. The woman felt as though she was in a trance and could hardly move.

This has all the hallmarks of a classic UFO case: electromagnetic effects, animal reactions, and physical effects on the witnesses. However, Hendry determined that the witnesses were looking at the crescent Moon (the "saucer") with Mars and Jupiter next to it (the "pulsating lights"). The dimming of the car park lights was caused by intermittent

Shining brightly in the sky, the planet Venus, seen here (left) with the moon at dawn, can be mistaken for a UFO.

mist which eventually obscured the Moon and planets. The rest of the report is a marvellous product of human imagination.

Meteors and Fireballs

Meteors are less easy to identify after the event because of their transient nature. Humans are as bad at estimating time as they are at estimating brightness and distance, and reports often exaggerate the duration for which a meteor was seen. Even people normally familiar with meteors can be fooled by unusually bright fireballs.

Here is an example quoted by Philip Klass in his book *UFOs Explained.* Pilots aboard a commercial jet flying at 39,000 ft over the United States in 1969 were reportedly buzzed in daylight at a distance of 300 ft by a formation of four objects emitting a blue-green flame. A military jet flying some miles behind the airliner reported a squadron of UFOs approaching that suddenly started to climb as if to avoid a collision.

At the same time as this UFO "encounter," a brilliant daylight fireball broke up into several flaming pieces over the United States, and there seems little doubt that this is what the pilots saw, despite the fact that it was actually over 100 miles away from them. So even experienced pilots can make major errors of identification and distance. That doesn't make them bad airmen, simply human.

EVALUATING THE AUTHOR'S ARGUMENTS:

Ridpath is an amateur astronomer who has written and edited books on the subject. How might his background influence his assessment of UFOs? Does this affect your opinion of his argument? Explain your answer.

UFOs Are Usually Balloons

"Research balloons fly extremely high and often display some unique characteristics when viewed from the ground."

Tim Printy

In the following selection Tim Printy explains his belief that lighted balloons and research balloons account for many UFO sightings. Balloons, Printy explains, have been known to soar high in the sky, reflect sunlight, wobble, and rotate. These features prompt civilians and pilots to report that they have seen a mysterious spaceship. Tim Printy is a UFO debunker—that is, someone who tries to prove that UFOs do not exist. He is an astrophotographer whose photos have appeared in publications such as *Astronomy* and *HB* (Hale Bopp) *Magazine*.

AS YOU READ, CONSIDER THE FOLLOWING QUESTIONS:
1. According to the viewpoint, what reasons did the first pilot give for his belief that the UFO was not a balloon?
2. In the author's contention, what are four characteristics of research balloons that may account for their being mistaken as UFOs?
3. What caused Mantell's death, in Printy's view?

Probably one of the most laughed at explanations for UFO reports is a weather balloon. It was presented that it was ridiculous for observers to misidentify such a common everyday object. It can be very easy as [UFO investigator] Alan Hendry found out. In his database of IFOs [identified flying objects], the number one source of daylight disc UFO reports was a balloon. This agrees with USAF [U.S. Air Force] figures that show that balloons often result in UFO reports.

Why do people misidentify balloons? Perhaps the best way to explain this is to describe each type of balloon and how case histories demonstrate the misperceptions involved. . . .

Weather Balloons

On September 24, 1952, a Navy TBM Avenger [aircraft] had [an] encounter with a light near Cuba. The pilot's report read:

> As it [the light] approached the city from the east it started a left turn. I started to intercept. During the first part of the chase the closest I got to the light was 8 to 10 miles. At this time it appeared to be as large as an SNJ [aircraft] and had a greenish tail that looked to be five to six times as long as the light's diameter. This tail was seen several times in the next 10 minutes in periods of from 5 to 30 seconds each. As I reached 10,000 feet it appeared to be at 15,000 feet and in a left turn. It took 40 degrees of bank to keep the nose of my plane on the light. At this time I estimated the light to be in a 10-to-15 mile orbit.
>
> At 12,000 feet I stopped climbing, but the light was still climbing faster than I was. I then reversed my turn from left to right and the light also reversed. As I was not gaining distance, I held a steady course south trying to estimate a perpendicular between the light and myself. The light was moving north, so I turned north. As I turned, the light appeared to move west, then south over the base. I again tried to intercept but the light appeared to climb rapidly at a 60 degree angle. It climbed to 35,000 feet, then started a rapid descent.
>
> Prior to this, while the light was still at approximately 15,000 feet, I deliberately placed it between the moon and myself three times

An atmospheric research balloon is launched into the daytime sky. Some UFO researchers claim that balloons are behind most daytime UFO sightings.

Two unidentified flying objects hovering over Palermo, Sicily, capture the attention of four bystanders in this 1954 photo.

to try to identify a solid body. I and my two crewmen all had a good view of the light as it passed the moon. We could see no solid body. We considered the fact that it might be an aerologist's balloon, but we did not see a silhouette. Also, we would have rapidly caught up with and passed a balloon.

During its descent, the light appeared to slow down at about 10,000 feet, at which time I made three runs on it. Two were on a 90 degree collision course, and the light traveled at tremendous speed across my bow. On the third run I was so close that the light blanked out the airfield below me. Suddenly it started a dive and I followed, losing it at 1,500 feet.

The following night the Navy sent the same pilot up and this time with a lighted [weather] balloon. The pilot was surprised to find that his "dogfight" was duplicated and the Navy wrote a rather long report for Project Bluebook [the Air Force's investigation of UFOs] on the event.

Looking at this description and comparing it to the Gorman case[1] we find similarities but it was already suspected that a lighted balloon was the cause. [Edward] Ruppelt writes [in *The Report on Unidentified Flying Objects*], *"Gorman fought a lighted balloon too. An analysis of the sighting by the Air Weather Service sent to ATIC* [which conducts experiments with balloons] *in a letter dated January 24, 1949, proved it."* This shows that pilots can easily be fooled by a balloon at night.

Can the same thing happen during the day? Considering the speeds involved, it would not be unheard of for a misidentification based on what I have previously stated. . . .

The Research Balloon

Research balloons fly extremely high and often display some unique characteristics when viewed from the ground. According to Hendry:

. . . due to reflected sunlight, resulting in descriptions like "line segment" and "angel with gown and wings" (seen through binoculars) and an "oval with lights on its corners.". . . Nothing particularly fancy was observed about the motion of these large research balloons. They either remained stationary or proceeded very slowly, since they were propelled entirely by the wind. They can be seen to move, stop, and move again (or descend, stop, descend); they are reported to "wobble"

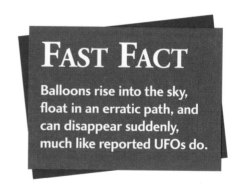

FAST FACT

Balloons rise into the sky, float in an erratic path, and can disappear suddenly, much like reported UFOs do.

very slowly, depending on tricks of reflected sunlight. The balloon can even appear to rotate. In one case a balloon was perceived to rock back and forth and another time to move randomly in and out of clouds.

Probably one of the most famous of the research balloon cases was that of pilot Thomas Mantell on January 7, 1948. That afternoon, reports

1. In 1948 Lieutenant George Gorman nearly collided with, and subsequently gave chase to, a UFO.

In 1948 U.S. Air Force pilot Thomas Mantell lost consciousness and crashed his plane while pursuing an unidentified flying object at high altitudes.

of a UFO began to come in for the state of Ohio. The UFO took on the following descriptions:

"Object appeared like 'ice-cream cone topped with red'—apparently white with red above."

"Like tear-drop—round; later, object seemed fluid."

"Round—at times cone shaped."

"It was very white and looked like an umbrella."

Four P-51 fighters happened to be on a ferry mission from Georgia about this time and its flight commander, Captain Thomas Mantell, was asked to investigate. Mantell saw the UFO and reported,

> I have an object in sight above and ahead of me and it appears to be moving at about half my speed. . . . It appears to be a metallic object or possibly reflection of sun from a metallic object and it is of tremendous size . . . directly ahead of me and slightly above . . . I am trying to close for a better look.

Mantell pursued the UFO to a high altitude. Unfortunately, Mantell did not have any oxygen for the altitudes he was attempting to reach. He passed out and then plummeted to his death. For many years the Mantell case was considered the planet Venus but Ed Ruppelt, the original head of Project Bluebook, was able to determine the actual cause, a Project Skyhook balloon. Despite this being published in the 1950s, Richard Hall's *UFOs: The Best Evidence,* published in the 1960s, still included this case as unsolved. Even more amazing is that some UFO databases continue to post this case as unidentified and other UFOlogists claim that the UFO attacked Mantell. The reason they do not buy the Skyhook explanation is they felt that Mantell would never have gone so high without oxygen. Numerous pilots have met their fate in the sky because of errors of this type. Mantell died due to his lack of using oxygen in an effort to pursue a high altitude spy/research balloon. . . .

Balloons, like stars, planes, meteors, etc. can and do generate UFO reports. Unfortunately, it seems that UFO investigators rarely appreciate balloons as a source. For a UFOlogist to state a UFO report was caused by a balloon is almost the same as saying Venus was the cause. This explanation often generates ridicule from UFOlogists and they will point out that witnesses could never have misperceived such a mundane event.

EVALUATING THE AUTHORS' ARGUMENTS:

The author of the viewpoint you just read accuses UFOlogists of ignoring reports that identify the actual nature of UFOs. After examining the evidence on both sides, do you think that the UFOs detailed in this chapter are extraterrestrial craft, or are they other, more common objects? Support your answer using facts from the viewpoints.

Some UFOs Are Natural Earth Lights

Paul Devereux

"Earth lights sometimes behave . . . like inquisitive animals."

Paul Devereux, a researcher of unusual geophysical phenomena, has written several books skeptical of UFOs, including *UFOs and UFOlogy.* In the following viewpoint he writes that some UFO sightings can be explained by a phenomenon that he calls earth lights. Geological and meteorological forces, such as stress in the earth's crust, can cause lights to appear in the atmosphere, explains Devereux. These lights can exert strange qualities, he says. They may produce magnetic fields that cause hallucinations in witnesses or can be visible from one side but not the other. These mysterious characteristics may make earth lights responsible for some UFO reports, Devereux concludes. This selection was adapted from a presentation given by Devereux at the Dana Centre Science Museum in London.

AS YOU READ, CONSIDER THE FOLLOWING QUESTIONS:

1. To what does Devereux attribute the majority of UFO sightings?

2. According to the author, what other civilizations have seen earth lights?
3. How does the author back up his claim that exotic phenomena like earth lights can still be eluding science?

First may I say that I think most UFO reports are the product of (i) misperception of mundane aerial objects whether man-made or astronomical; (ii) mirage effects; (iii) hoax; (iv) psychosocial effects ranging from mental aberration to temporary personal stress conditions affecting a witness's perception or interpretation of a perception; (v) the occurrence (unawares) in the witness of trance conditions, such as when awaking from or falling into sleep, or when

An artist's rendition of ball lightning shows a glowing orb moving erratically through the sky. Some witnesses might mistake such natural lights for a UFO.

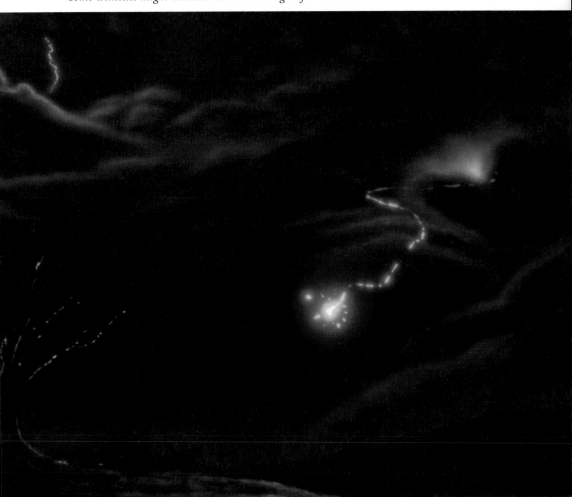

driving, especially at night. Of all these, I'd suggest simple misperception is by far the greatest cause, though I suspect the trance explanation is involved more than we might suppose, especially in the case of reported alien abductions.

Earth Lights Are Mysterious

Having said all that—as a result of my own *experience* as well as my own research—I ALSO think there is a small *rump* or residue of sighting reports that DO actually relate to genuinely unexplained phenomena. In my opinion, a percentage of this small rump of sightings relates to geophysical or meteorological phenomena that I have termed 'earth lights'. These seem to be exotic natural phenomena apparently belonging to the same family as earthquake lights and ball lightning but with their own distinctive characteristics, such as sometimes displaying greater longevity than earthquake lights or ball lightning.

This image was taken from a video that captured a series of rapidly moving bright lights in the skies over Campeche, Mexico, in 2004.

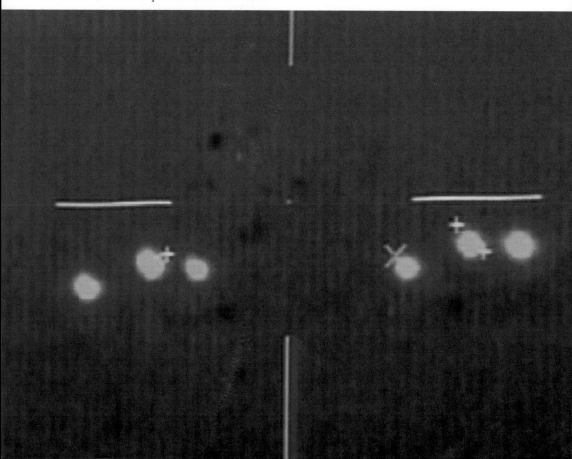

There certainly seems to be an association between the appearance of earth lights and factors such as stresses and strains in the earth's crust, but these do not have to amount to earthquakes as such—for instance, evidence suggests that the pressure of bodies of water on underlying geology can provide sufficient tectonic forces to produce luminosities in the atmosphere. And there are doubtless many more sources of energy, geological and meteorological, that could power these lightforms. We simply do not yet know for sure, nor do we know how the lights keep coherent forms and apparently move about, but that is true too of ball lightning. I suspect that these phenomena have much to teach our physicists, especially when we learn to look for them and study them without prejudice—on the one hand the prejudice of overly-conservative scientism, or, on the other hand, the prejudice of those who insist on an extra-terrestrial explanation. We must always be aware that 'UFOlogy' is not the same thing as the UFOs, the phenomena, themselves.

FAST FACT

Earth lights may appear as orbs of light, luminous vapors, spheres with fiery tails, or flames. They can look blue, yellow, orange, amber, white, or sometimes red or green. They can last a few seconds to several minutes.

(And, incidentally, the question as to whether there is other intelligent life in the universe has nothing directly to do with whether or not UFOs exist or are extra-terrestrial craft. It is a red herring that often gets into the argument about UFOs. There could be a billion alien civilisations across the universe without any of them having visited our planet.) . . .

Earth Lights Throughout History

'Earth lights' are or were known to traditional and ancient peoples: they were fairies to the Irish and other Celtic peoples, though also harbingers of death known as 'corpse candles' to the Welsh; the disembodied heads of women who had died in childbirth to Malaysians; the lanterns of the *chota admis,* the little men, according to the people of the Darjeeling area; manifestations of Bodhisattvas to Chinese and Tibetan Buddhists, who built temples where such sightings

In this photo, sunlight refracted by ice crystals in the air appears as a halo surrounding a pine tree. This phenomenon could conceivably be mistaken as a UFO sighting.

occurred; they were devils to people in western Africa, and so on and so forth.

But can exotic phenomena like these still be eluding science? Well, why not—look at the recent discoveries of gigantic light phenomena like ELVES, a discoid type lightning of enormous size, and SPRITES, multi-coloured discharges of energy rising thousands of feet above some thunder clouds. And remember, science still cannot adequately explain ball lightning!

Behavior of Earth Lights

What are earth lights? Well they certainly have electrical and magnetic attributes, and some form of plasma [a cloud of highly charged particles] is assumed. Modern witnesses who come close to earth lights typically report hallucinatory episodes—suggesting magnetic fields that are known to be able to affect parts of the brain. One thing that has struck me in poring over witness reports from different periods of time and parts of the world is the similarity of descriptions stating that earth lights sometimes behave as if they have a rudimentary intelligence, like inquisitive animals. (Intriguingly, it was very recently announced that scientists in Rumania had created laboratory plasmas that they observed behaved exactly like living cells.) Another type of observation noted in witnesses' reports from all times and places that has impressed me is that the lights sometimes display illogical effects, such as, and particularly, being visible from one side but not the other. This makes me suspect that earth lights may be *macro-quantal* events—phenomena that should exist only at the sub-atomic quantum level, but have somehow manifested on our larger macro-scale of experience. More modest macro-quantal phenomena have already been produced in the laboratory, and I think earth lights, produced in the greatest laboratory of them all (the one that belongs to Mother Nature) have remarkable lessons to teach us.

EVALUATING THE AUTHOR'S ARGUMENTS:

The author is a scientific researcher. Describe how his credentials might inform his argument that natural phenomena are responsible for UFO sightings.

Chapter 2

Have Humans Been Abducted by UFOs?

A UFO abducts a human being with a powerful beam of light in this illustration.

Humans Have Been Abducted by UFOs

Matthew Graeber

"*Many abductees do report suffering quite a bit of traumatic abuse at the hands of the aliens.*"

According to Matthew Graeber in the following viewpoint, UFOs pursue humans in order to capture and perform tests on them. Graeber outlines cases in which people claim to have been chased by unfriendly UFOs. During such experiences abductees are subjected to abuse and medical examinations that cause great fear and pain, Graeber claims. He uses these stories to argue that humans are justified in their fear of being abducted by aliens. Graeber founded the UFO Report and Information Center in Philadelphia, and served as its director for eight years.

AS YOU READ, CONSIDER THE FOLLOWING QUESTIONS:

1. What was the reported cause of Betty Cash's death, as Graeber puts it?
2. What fault does the author find with suggestions by UFO researchers that the Bouchard family was abducted by aliens?
3. According to the author, how have people been physically affected by close contact with UFOs?

UFOs are . . . believed to produce (or induce) some unusual effects on the individuals who have come into close proximity with them. While many of these effects are thought to be beneficial, still others represent an array of emotional and physical injuries such as burns, skin blistering, eye irritations, partial paralysis, and the loss of hair—all assumed to be caused by the UFO propulsion system's emissions or its weaponry.

Perhaps the best documented of all the residual-effects cases is that of Mrs. Betty Cash's encounter with a large, diamond-shaped, heat-producing UFO that was apparently being pursued by a swarm of military helicopters. According to Mrs. Cash, her friend Vickie Landrum, and Vickie's grandson, Colby (who also witnessed the event), Mrs. Cash developed a number of lingering medical problems after their close encounter and wrote to various governmental and military agencies with the hope of identifying the object that she, Vickie, Colby, and several others had been exposed to on that fateful night (December 29, 1980) in Huffman, Texas.

Mrs. Cash passed away on the 18th anniversary of her UFO encounter, reportedly from complications of the injuries that she suffered from exposure to (radioactive?) UFO emissions.

A man exhibits a grid pattern of burn marks on his stomach after he allegedly approached a UFO in Manitoba, Canada, in 1967.

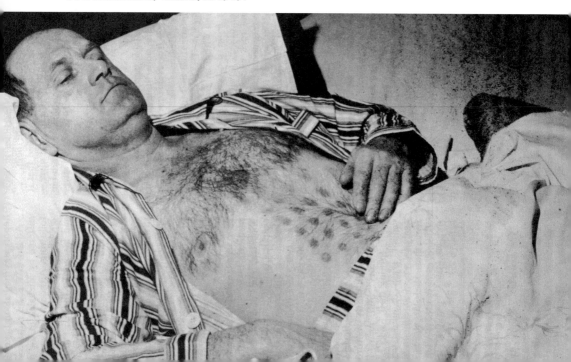

This painting shows Betty Cash and Vickie and Colby Landrum as they approach a diamond-shaped alien ship surrounded by military helicopters.

Pursued by a UFO

Approaching speeds of 92 miles per hour, a young nurse in New Jersey attempted to elude a speeding UFO that suddenly appeared at the right rear of her car and relentlessly followed her at an estimated altitude of 100 feet above the tree-lined roadway and just 50 feet behind her vehicle. She heard no sound. The UFO appeared to be a convex, disk-like craft with an array of rapidly flashing lights along its outer edge.

When questioned about her experience, the young woman exclaimed, "Ya know, I was really scared to death that they were going to catch me . . . I mean, because they do all those horrible things to people that they abduct."

Thus she informed the field investigator that she was fully aware of the abduction scenario, which is often characterized by abject fear and the infliction of physical pain. But had this driver lost control of her vehicle, crashed, and died at the scene of the accident, police investigators would have had no idea that she had been pursued by a UFO or that her fear of being captured by aliens were contributing factors to the mishap.

"I'm gonna have to write you up, buddy. Now I suppose you're gonna claim you didn't know this planet is restricted to 'abduct and release' only."

Obviously, the young lady's fears are not unfounded, because many abductees do report suffering quite a bit of traumatic abuse at the hands of the aliens during the so-called "medical examination" phase of the abduction experience. While many individuals may feel that they really would like to be taken on board a UFO by extraterrestrials, many others shudder at the very thought of experiencing such an ordeal.

Abducted by a UFO?

On November 8, 1973, a young Canadian couple and their three small children were followed by a light-encrusted UFO that chased their light truck for several miles. The couple attempted to elude capture and exited Highway 417 at Russell Road in Ottawa. Mr. and Mrs. Rick Bouchard described the UFO as a disk that wobbled like a duck (a commonly reported UFO flight characteristic) as it flew just above the roadway directly behind their vehicle. Reportedly, the craft even lit up the interior of an overpass that they coursed through in the darkness. The shaken couple described their experience as "harrowing" and something which they and their children would never forget. Subsequent investigative inquiries into the matter by Canadian and American UFO researchers suggest that the entire family may have been abducted—although neither Bouchard, his wife, or their children seemed to have any conscious recollection of seeing the UFO beyond the Russell Road Exit point.

UFO literature is replete with similar pursuit cases involving autos, trucks, motorcycles, and aircraft of various types. In some cases, the auto's ignition system is reported to malfunction or the aircraft's inflight instrumentation suddenly goes haywire. It's quite possible that some fatalities seemingly attributable to human error and equipment failure may actually have been the result of a UFO pursuit that took a tragic turn. . . .

The Abduction Phenomenon

It appears that a silent segment of our society may be negatively affected by the UFO/abduction phenomenon, as well as by the media coverage and portrayal of its overall character—generally shown as being frightening and traumatic. Many UFO experts and abduction experiencers would have us believe that there is a beneficial and transformational lesson in the pain and fear associated with alien abductions. Still, people fear enduring

> # FAST FACT
>
> In 1992, MIT (Massachusetts Institute of Technology) held a week-long Abduction Study Conference that resulted in over 700 pages of case studies and evidence of alien abductions.

such an experience. They reject the notion that being selected for alien cross-breeding experimentation is something to be desired.

Perhaps those who fear capture by advanced intelligences from the stars are having totally justified reactions to the threat and abuse that interfacing with such little monsters may really represent. After all, if Earthlings kidnap and abuse other Earthlings, it is a serious criminal offense punishable by prolonged periods of incarceration. Are we to seriously assume that "advanced intelligences" from outer space have no such concept of law? . . .

Some UFOs Remain Unaccounted For

Over 50 years of intense UFO interest, investigation, researching, evaluation, and theorizing by countless UFO aficionados have enabled today's field investigators to better examine, evaluate, and identify many of the unusual airborne objects that are being reported. Yet a small percentage of the reports continue to elude positive identification.

Many of these unknowns reportedly exhibit behavior that is thought to be indicative of volition and so-called physics-defying aerobatics. But after all these years, the objective UFO research community still does not know what that means or even if these reported UFO behaviors can be positively linked to nuts-and-bolt devices originating from an unknown earthly location, another world, or even another dimension.

EVALUATING THE AUTHOR'S ARGUMENTS:

The author of this viewpoint believes that humans have been abducted by UFOs. Considering what you know on this topic, do you agree? Explain your answer.

There Is No Credible Evidence of UFO Abductions

Jim Giglio and Scott Snell

"When one is investigating a UFO incident . . . critical thinking should be strenuously applied. But . . . this does not appear to be happening."

According to Jim Giglio and Scott Snell in the viewpoint that follows, aliens do not visit or abduct humans. The authors argue that the evidence of alien visitation is poor. It consists mainly of incoherent statements made by witnesses who are not likely credible. In the authors' view, UFO believers fail to think critically about this problem and are too quick to accept poor evidence as true. Giglio and Snell conclude that people who report alien abductions actually describe extraterrestrials they have seen on popular TV shows and movies. Giglio and Snell are board members of the National Capital Area Skeptics, an organization that encourages critical thinking about UFOs.

AS YOU READ, CONSIDER THE FOLLOWING QUESTIONS:
1. What issues do Giglio and Snell take with the UFO statement submitted to the National UFO Reporting Center in 1999?
2. How do the authors define the missing time phenomenon?
3. In the authors' opinion, what television series formed the basis for Barney Hill's alien abduction story?

Examine the [UFO] sighting report that [UFO researcher] Richard Dolan regards as typical and informative. The report was submitted to the National UFO Reporting Center in 1999 and refers to an event that allegedly occurred in 1976 near Hydes, Maryland:

> it was dusk that day. we saw this round craft come out of the northeast over the horizon. it was slowly rotating counter clockwise. white lights only, were on the outer edges. it moved slowly, maybe 30 to 40 miles per hour. it came directly over us. we were on a horse farm, laying on the front lawn just after dinner. this craft was just below the sunlight that was left in the sky. we could not see any details. when it came over us, it stopped. then separated into four smaller craft, then at the blink of an eye, they shot over the horizon. each ship went directly north, south, east and west respectively. there was absolutely no sound from this craft. we learned the next day that there were sightings over peachbottom atomic plant that day. the same direction that our craft came from. to this day, we have never spoken about this to anyone, not even between ourselves. there were 6 of us. two music teachers, a medical lab tech, a texas instruments tech, police officer, a kindergarten teacher.

Errors in Logic

As scientific evidence, this statement has numerous "red flags" hanging all over it. The writer, supposedly a professional, seems not to want to bother with the standard capitalization rules for English sentences. The statement is only semi-coherent, with sentences describing various aspects of the incident tumbling over each other in a rush; with 23 years to think about the incident, it ought to have been possible to organize the description into a coherent narrative. (S)he reports that no details of the object could be seen, yet states that it was 1000 feet in diameter and traveling 30 or 40 miles per hour. How these size and speed determinations were made is unspecified, nor is there an explanation for an inability to resolve details when it *was* possible to determine size and speed. Accepting the size and speed estimates leads to another problem. Hydes, Maryland is located near a number of heavily-traveled highways and air transportation corridors. Near-by observers should have numbered in the thousands and generated numerous newspaper headlines; we are referred, instead, to some alleged sightings at a nuclear power plant located a considerable distance away.

Mr. Dolan informs us that this kind of report is typical. He's quite right; it *is* typical, but as scientific evidence it's worthless. Individuals

Photographs of UFOs such as this one are often grainy and of poor quality and some are proven to be hoaxes.

and organizations adhering to the notion of ET visitation accumulate reports like this by the thousands and periodically present them to the public to support their position. There's a logical fallacy at work in this constant piling-up of reports, the fallacy that large amounts of bad evidence somehow add up to good evidence. They don't. You can't make a silk purse out of a sow's ear, nor can you make one out of 10,000 sow's ears. The Colorado investigators were right; despite their volume, reports such as this, which had contributed nothing to science as of 1968, have yet to contribute anything in the intervening 33 years.

The fact that Mr. Dolan gives credence to this flawed statement illustrates an aspect of the UFO issue that ought to trouble proponents of the notion that this issue is a serious scientific problem. We refer to an apparent unwillingness, on the part of far too many of these proponents, to apply even a modicum of critical thinking to such reports.

Possible Hoaxes

One of us (Scott) recently attended a UFO conference. At this event, a physicist widely considered to be a technically adept investigator (who

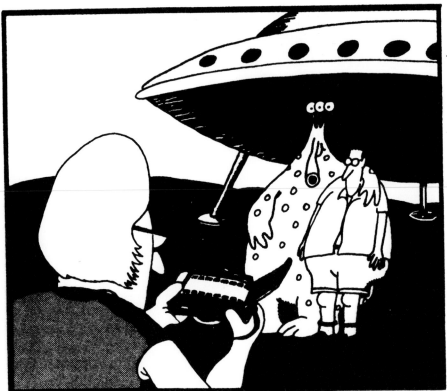

"Yes, yes, already, Warren! . . . There *is* film in the camera!"

shall remain nameless) gave a presentation in which he described his analysis of photos showing peculiar lights over the night skyline of an Arizona city [Phoenix]. He showed the audience how he had compared the lights of the city in the two different photos that the witness claimed had been taken only a few moments apart. There was no question that the city lights had changed markedly. Test photos taken for comparison showed that one was taken sometime before 11 P.M. and the other taken sometime afterwards, despite the witness's claim that both were taken in quick succession at about 8 P.M. (At about 11 P.M., skyline lighting changes significantly as businesses and homes turn off their lights for the night.) The

investigator then asked the witness for the photographic negatives. He learned that the two photos were actually from *different rolls of film*, separated by several other frames, some showing only the skyline, some showing only the peculiar "UFO" lights. (This aspect of the report is striking in its resemblance to the [University of] Colorado [Condon] Report's Case #7.)

At this point, a listener to the talk might have expected the investigator to conclude that this was not a reliable case to proceed with. The witness's story did not jibe with the photographic facts, and the contents of the interim photos suggested experiments in trick photography. But the listener would have been wrong. The investigator touted this as "missing time discovered through photo analysis." (For the uninitiated, the "missing time" phenomenon is a standard component of alien abduction stories; it occurs when someone notices that the time on a clock or watch is considerably later than expected; the abduction event that supposedly occupied this time is somehow erased from memory.)

When questioned as to his conclusions, the investigator stressed that ". . . the witness is a very credible, respected member of her community. She would not have lied about it." Apparently this investigator

One of the most famous alien abduction accounts is that of Betty and Barney Hill (inset) of New Hampshire. In 1967 they claimed to have interacted with aliens on a UFO.

had never read Colorado case 7; that hoaxer was a retired military officer with an "irreproachable" reputation. The investigator also apparently never heard of Occam's Razor, the principle which states that, other factors being equal, one chooses the simpler of two competing explanations for an observation.

When one is investigating a UFO incident in the expectation that it might provide evidence that our planet is being visited by ET's (a most extraordinary hypothesis), a high level of critical thinking should be strenuously applied. But in the two examples of "pro-UFO" evidence seen here, this does not appear to be happening. . . .

The "Standard Model" Alien

There is also compelling evidence that the appearance of UFO occupants, as widely accepted among "contact" adherents, arose out of a particular episode of a television series. Barney Hill, who was allegedly abducted by beings from a UFO in the early 1960s (the initial case of this type), went into therapy and was hypnotized in the course of his treatment. Under hypnosis, Hill described the eyes of his abductors as "speaking." This peculiar phrase had been used by an extraterrestrial character in an episode of the ABC-TV series "The Outer Limits," which had aired only days before Hill's hypnosis session. The episode was "The Bellero Shield"; the alien portrayed was bald, essentially featureless in face and body, and had swept-back eyes, just as Hill sketched under hypnosis. Although other early reports of UFO occupants varied significantly from Hill's (probably inspired by other stereotypical alien images), his description is the one that has saturated popular culture via the media.

In 1975, NBC-TV broadcast a dramatization of Hill's experience in a made-for-TV film called "The UFO Incident." Many millions of people watched this allegedly true story and learned what aliens are supposed to look like. A couple of years later, Steven Spielberg's "Close Encounters of the Third Kind" became one of the most popular motion pictures ever made, depicting beings similar to those in Hill's description. Public perception of the "standard model" alien was further influenced by the cover of the 1987 best-selling book "Communion," an allegedly true account of alien contact, which sported the expected image. Had Barney Hill's hypnosis session taken place earlier, or had the ABC network scheduled the "Bellero Shield" later, we would in all likelihood have a different "standard model" alien. . . .

The Burden of Proof

In closing, a final point: The arguments made here are not conclusive. We cannot say with certainty that our planet is not being visited. We can, however, note that those who support the idea of ET visitation have always had a heavy burden of proof, a burden that has only grown heavier as time has passed. We skeptics, who find this idea implausible, have a lighter burden, and it gets lighter with time.

EVALUATING THE AUTHORS' ARGUMENTS:

Giglio and Snell argue that no compelling evidence of UFOs has ever been found. If physical proof of alien abductions *was* found, would you be more likely to believe that such occurrences are real? What type of evidence would you find most convincing? Why or why not?

UFO Abductions Are Delusions

Joe Nickell, interviewed by
John C. Snider

"The fantasy prone person may . . . see an alien, and receive special messages from the Space Brothers."

The following viewpoint is from an interview with Joe Nickell, who has authored books and articles that are skeptical of paranormal phenomena. He is interviewed by John C. Snider, editor of the online science fiction magazine scifi*dimensions*. In the interview Nickell explains how people can be led to believe they have been abducted by aliens. Exposure to science fiction literature and movies, undergoing hypnosis, and having a fantasy prone personality can lead to such delusions, Nickell claims. Some people's abduction delusion even leads them to look for—and find—physical marks or implants from alien experimentation. But Nickell says these can be attributed to a rational and explainable cause.

AS YOU READ, CONSIDER THE FOLLOWING QUESTIONS:
1. Which three books by Whitley Strieber are mentioned by the author?
2. In Nickell's view, hypnosis is an "invitation" to do what?
3. Name four traits of fantasy prone people, according to Nickell.

Scifidimensions: What, really, is the origin of the modern UFO phenomenon?

Joe Nickell: Well, there have always been strange sights in the sky, and of course you can trace those back to biblical times and beyond, but people tended in ancient times to see these as omens, or signs and portents. But in modern times we begin to get, by the late nineteenth century, in the 1890s, something called The Great Airship Mystery. These were reports that giant airships were traveling across the US, and there were elaborate stories, eyewitness accounts and so forth. Some of these were no doubt journalistic hoaxes, and some of it was hype, and who knows what else, maybe some fantasies of imaginative people. But it appears that there were no airships in the sky in the 1890s! So it's a lesson in mass delusion, and what scientists might call "contagion", but an interesting kind of forerunner, because there were ideas of airships in the science fiction literature. . . .

I think you could almost always show that whatever trend you've seen in the so-called real world has been anticipated in science fic-

Pictured is a still from the 1977 movie Close Encounters of the Third Kind, *which inspired popular interest in the alien abduction phenomenon.*

tion. It could be shown that there were alien abductions in [the science fiction magazine] *Amazing Stories* long before that was ever really reported.

Didn't UFO reports jump dramatically when the movie Close Encounters of the Third Kind *[about alien sightings] came out?*

I'm sure that they did. There's almost no doubt that any kind of advertisement for a phenomenon will increase our expectation, will have people going outdoors and looking up at the sky; and, of course, if you look at the sky a lot, sooner or later, something unusual will happen— a meteor, or a upper-atmospheric research balloon, or a secret test craft or something. If enough people are looking at the sky more and more, and there are more and more things in the sky because of our technological age, they will coincide and we'll have sightings. . . .

FAST FACT

Research on memory has shown that people can be persuaded to believe they had past experiences that never occurred.

Delusion and Waking Dreams

I wanted to talk about a man named Whitley Strieber [a science fiction and fantasy author who has written a series of nonfiction books, the first of which is entitled Communion *].*

Communion, and later *Communion Letters,* and *Confirmation,* several books . . .

He claims that he has had a life-long "relationship", for lack of a better term, with what people know as the Grays, the short, big-eyed aliens, and that they have abducted him throughout his life. . . .

Do you think that Whitley Strieber is—is he a con man, is he delusional, or is he just a fantasy author with an over-active imagination?

It's hard to know what's in anybody's mind. I'm asked this all the time, is so-and-so sincere, or do they really think they talk to ghosts, or whatever. I don't have much of a way to know that. You just have to look at the evidence. If you look at *Communion,* and you look at the experiences that Strieber describes, he describes a rather typical and classic experience known as a waking dream. A waking dream is a phenomenon that exists in the twilight zone between waking and sleeping. . . .

"IF THAT ISN'T MY IMAGINATION, I'D BE SCARED STIFF!"

Sandy. © by Sandy. Reproduced by permission of Rothco Cartoons, Inc.

It's amazing how many people wrote him letters after they read his book, telling about having experiences themselves, and they describe experiences that are oftentimes these waking dreams. Now, that's not an explanation for *all* alien abduction cases. Some of those are done under hypnosis, which is an invitation to fantasize. . . .

The Yellow Brick Road to Fantasyland

Speaking of hypnosis . . . there are a number of people around the country (maybe worldwide) that make a living working with people who claim to have experienced abductions. As a matter of fact, I believe Whitley Strieber includes as an addendum to his first book Communion, *an affidavit from a psychologist who certifies that his hypnosis session with Whitley Strieber was legitimate and that the memories that he retrieved were sincere.*

Well, yeah, what happens with these abductees, and I remember when I first heard about alien abductions, and my reaction was like that of many skeptics: "Are these people crazy, or are they charlatans looking for attention?" That's a false dichotomy, because in my experience most of these people are sane, normal, and sincere. They have had a "real experience." It may be a waking dream, or it may be a hypnotic confabulation. I define it as the yellow brick road to fantasyland. Hypnosis is an invitation to go into a fantasy, and some people do it better than others. There are highly imaginative people (maybe 4% of

In this poster advertising a 1956 science fiction film, hordes of flying saucers and aliens launch an all-out assault on the human race.

the American public) that are so highly imaginative that they're called "fantasy prone." These people will have, probably, more of those waking dreams I mentioned. They also may have—and I say may, because there are a number of characteristics of fantasy-proneness. All of us have some of them, I'm sure. It'd be unusual if you didn't have *any* of them. You'd be a very dull person. If you have lots of the traits, you see, then we call it fantasy prone. It's not a difference so much in kind as degree. Some of the traits would include having an imaginary playmate as a child. Many of us have these, but grow out of them. The fantasy prone person may grow to have an adult version of that. They may, for example, talk to the Virgin Mary, or have a personal guardian angel over their shoulder . . . or see an alien, and receive special messages from the Space Brothers. If they didn't tell you about this, if they didn't mention this particular thing, you'd find them very normal people. They just wouldn't tell you about their contact with a space alien. And so, these are markers—being easily hypnotized, for example, having frequent out of body experiences, having vivid waking dreams or other vivid dreams. A number of these characteristics and the intensity of them indicate, perhaps, a fantasizing personality. . . .

Explaining Physical Evidence of Abductions

What about the people who claim that they have physical evidence? You've seen people who show scars, burns—there are people who even claim (I think Strieber might be among them) that small objects are in their body? What do you make of that?

Well . . . do you know that during the witchcraft craze in the sixteenth and seventeenth century, when there were people out looking for witches . . . one of the things you could do was, you could look for a witch's mark on someone. And it turns out that almost anything can be a witch's mark—a birthmark, a strange birthmark, or a hairy mole, or almost anything might be the witch's mark. If you sort of start with the mania that there are witches and you're going looking for a witch's mark you'll find *something*. I was on a TV show with one young woman who had these strange scars, and I saw them, and I know for a fact that her dermatologist diagnosed them as ordinary, common stretch marks.

And she ignored him?

Yeah, you know, maybe she had some dream or something, and now she thinks she's been abducted. If you strip yourself nude, and search your body, you may find an odd scar that you've forgotten about, or a strange marking. Some people have some kind of little object—but again, there's no pattern to these. I've seen one that looked like a little broken-off piece of sharp plastic or something that you might have gotten, say, as a childhood accident stepping on something, and forgot about it. It healed over and you forgot about it. Some of these may be little nodules of calcium that the body produces, or some other little glitch. There's certainly no scientific evidence that's been presented in a reasonable forum that suggests that any of these implants are extraterrestrial in origin.

EVALUATING THE AUTHORS' ARGUMENTS:

Nickell maintains that the UFO phenomenon is rooted in science fiction literature, concluding that alien experiences are not real. Do you find his argument more or less effective than that of Graeber, the first author in this chapter? Why?

Alien Abductions Are Sleep Hallucinations

Andrew D. Reisner

"The victim is essentially experiencing a dream phenomenon while awake."

Andrew D. Reisner is a clinical psychologist at Cambridge Psychiatric Hospital in Ohio. In the viewpoint that follows, he suggests that people who believe they have been visited or kidnapped by aliens are actually hallucinating. Such hallucinations occur as a person is just falling asleep or waking up. He discusses a man named John who thought that at night he was being abducted by aliens and visited by a demon. After his admittance into a psychiatric hospital, John realized that his encounters were the result of this dream phenomenon, Reisner reports. He suspects that most people who believe they have been snatched by aliens are not mentally ill but are likely suffering from sleep hallucinations.

AS YOU READ, CONSIDER THE FOLLOWING QUESTIONS:

1. What happens during "hypnopompic" or "hypnagogic" hallucinations, according to the author?

2. What does Reisner imply may have promoted John to see the alien at age twenty-six?

3. What is Wicca, as the author puts it?

A s [astronomer and UFO skeptic] Carl Sagan suggested, we humans are never far from the realm of the irrational despite the buffer of science and reason. Normal people can come uncomfortably close to this irrational realm when they are either half awake or half asleep, and experience either hypnagogic or hypnopompic hallucinations. In these relatively common and normal experiences, a person may be temporarily unable to move, a state known as sleep paralysis, and may experience vivid hallucinations either when first falling asleep (hypnagogic hallucinations), or upon awakening (hypnopompic hallucinations).

It can be a terrifying experience, leaving the person wondering not only about the reality of what they have seen, but also about their own sanity. The hallucinations seem very real. This phenomenon is thought to occur due to a benign but abnormal transition between sleep and wakefulness. The victim is essentially experiencing a dream phenomenon while awake, and is unable to move, because during sleep, the body's movement is partially inhibited in order to prevent people from getting up and acting out their dreams. Hypnagogic and hypnopompic hallucinations are thought to be the culprit in many paranormal phenomena, including nocturnal visits from aliens and ghosts and demons.

John's Case History

Ignorance of, and misunderstandings about, these types of normal hallucinations may cause unnecessary anxiety, or even play a significant role in the onset and progress of severe psychiatric symptoms, as in the case of John, a 36-year-old employed, married man. John's difficulties started innocently enough. When he was five or six years old, while trying to get to sleep, he saw a little man in his room who was about six inches tall. John saw the little man go in and out of a door in the room. Later, at age twenty-six, after reading a popular book on UFO abduction [by Whitley Strieber], John woke up, unable to move,

This illustration depicts an alien with the physical characteristics most often described by witnesses: dark, slanting eyes and an oversized head.

and saw a four-foot-tall, gray visitor, resembling the prototypic alien described in Strieber's book. This led to some speculation on John's part that he may have been abducted by aliens, perhaps more than once. The only adverse social or psychological consequence of this experience was that when he told others about it, and his speculations, he endured some teasing.

Under stress a few years later, John had more experiences of awakening in a paralyzed state and seeing a taller, dark and menacing visitor—one so tall it reached the top of a doorway. The apparition, moreover, wore a wide-brimmed black hat and black cloak, resembling characters from movies he had recently seen depicting "Zorro" and "The Shadow." John considered, however, that the apparition "might be a demon."

Some years later things took a turn for the worse when . . . John fell into a deep depression and seriously considered suicide.

John developed a friendship with Judy, a devotee of Wicca, a religion involving the worship of nature and the practice of "white magic." After long talks and the exchange of personal paranormal experiences, the two friends became convinced that John's recent visitor was a demon. . . .

Interpreting John's "Paranormal" Experiences

[After John was hospitalized following several more hallucinations,] John's depression and psychotic thinking had cleared, and he saw his unusual experiences in a more rational light. Possibly, what began as a

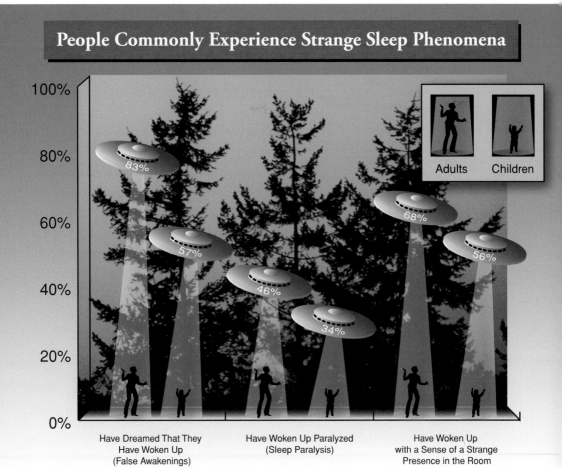

People Commonly Experience Strange Sleep Phenomena

Adults	Children	

100%
83%
80%
68%
57%
60%
56%
46%
40%
34%
20%
0%

Have Dreamed That They Have Woken Up (False Awakenings)

Have Woken Up Paralyzed (Sleep Paralysis)

Have Woken Up with a Sense of a Strange Presence in the Room

Source: Susan Blackmore, *Skeptical Inquirer,* May/June 1998.

mid-life crisis in an emotionally vulnerable, suggestible, imaginative man turned into a serious depression accompanied by a loss of contact with reality. This was fueled, no doubt, by a misinterpretation of his hypnopompic hallucinations, which had received consensual validation from his friend's paranormal interpretation of the events.

Once in a psychiatric hospital, and separated from occult and paranormal views, the concepts of sleep paralysis and hypnagogic and hypnopompic hallucinations were offered, and John readily accepted them as the best explanation for his unusual experiences. In a way, John's suggestibility was working in his favor. I had him read a few pages on the topic of hypnagogic hallucinations from a book on investigation and debunking paranormal phenomena [by Robert Baker and Joe Nickell], and he stated that he intended to obtain and read the entire book. . . . John now saw clearly just how he had become a victim of misinterpretation and suggestion, and he swore it would never happen again.

At the time of his discharge from the second six-day hospitalization, John was essentially free of depression and psychosis, as well as from suicidal and homicidal thoughts. . . .

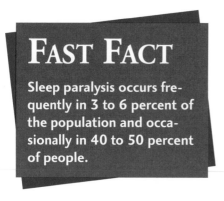

FAST FACT

Sleep paralysis occurs frequently in 3 to 6 percent of the population and occasionally in 40 to 50 percent of people.

Sleep Hallucinations in Many Cultures

The varied, and at times culture-bound, content of alien and demonic hallucinations provides another clue that such phenomena originate in the mind or brain, rather than being actual visitations from elsewhere. Hypnagogic images can be as simple as balls of light, or as apparently nonspiritual as an electrified telephone cord, [or, according to researchers Peter McKellar and L. Simpson,] "bright green frogs", "colored trees", or "a ship in a storm." Among a sample of Japanese [studied by K. Fukuda and associates], one man awoke paralyzed and " . . . saw a figure, which resembled a Buddhist image, on my stomach." People from other cultures may see "spiritual" images more in keeping with their own cultural expectations. Although [psychologist Ronald] Siegel notes some similarities in different historical

Some researchers maintain that alien abductions are merely sleep hallucinations.

culture's experience of the "succubus" [female demon] variant of the nightly intruder, he explains these similarities partly in terms of the half-asleep victim's brain attempting to make sense of common physiological stimuli that occur during sleep paralysis, perhaps in combination with "a return to the frightening, looming shapes of the infant's perceptual world."

When people in different cultures are awakened, paralyzed, and see, hear, and/or feel an ominous presence, some type of explanation will always be sought by those afflicted. In different cultures, and at other historical times, hypnagogic hallucinations were considered to be attacks by spirits such as incubi, succubi, Lilith, [what Siegel calls] "Mares," or [what Baker refers to as] "Old Hags." Interestingly, in the previously noted Japanese sample, 45 percent reportedly experienced an apparent variant of sleep paralysis, which was sometimes accompanied by hallucinations, and many of the subjects believed that evil spirits were involved with these attacks. Lacking accurate information about sleep paralysis with hypnagogic or hypnopompic hallucinations, it is easy to see why people look for supernatural and extraterrestrial explanations for such frightening and confusing phenomena. . . .

The Most Logical Explanation

What price might people pay when they are unaware of scientific explanations for visitations by aliens and demons? Since the experience of hypnagogic or hypnopompic phenomena is quite common, and since people often attribute supernatural causes to these experiences, from a statistical standpoint, it is not "abnormal" to engage in such spiritualistic speculation. Moreover, there is also evidence that people who believe that they have been abducted by aliens are, in general, not mentally ill. While there is evidence of some emotional difficulties among people who claim UFO abduction, others insist that [what UFOlogist Budd Hopkins and his associates call] "genuine UFO abductees" may suffer symptoms of post-traumatic stress disorder. The likelihood, however, that these people were truly abducted has been called into question, and in most cases, hypnagogic and hypnopompic hallucinations provide a better explanation.

EVALUATING THE AUTHORS' ARGUMENTS:

This author offers one detailed case study to argue that alien abduction experiences are sleep hallucinations. Matthew Graeber, the author of the first viewpoint in this chapter, uses several brief examples to illustrate his claim that aliens abduct humans. Which type of evidence do you find more convincing, and why?

Chapter 3

What Might Alien-Human Contact Be Like?

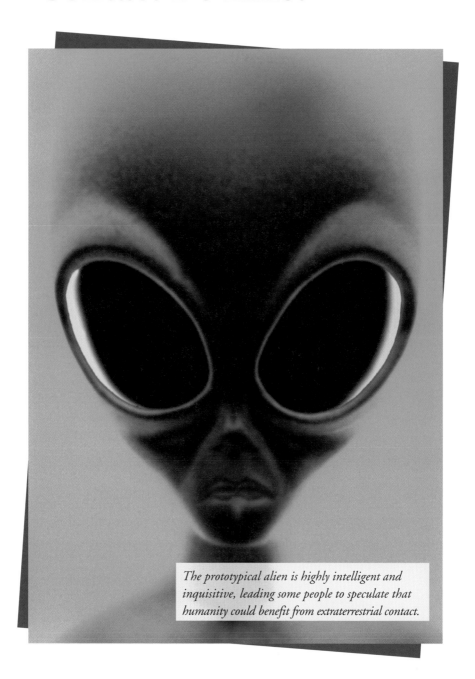

The prototypical alien is highly intelligent and inquisitive, leading some people to speculate that humanity could benefit from extraterrestrial contact.

Extraterrestrials Would Not Visit Earth

Seth Shostak

"The evidence has so far failed to convince me that [aliens] . . . have emissaries on our planet."

In the following viewpoint, Seth Shostak argues it is highly unlikely that aliens would travel hundreds or thousands of light-years to visit Earth. First, an extraterrestrial visit to Earth would be extremely rare, he says. This would cast doubt on claims that our planet has been visited in the past. It would also make it unlikely that Earth has been dropped in on numerous times before, he reasons. Countering claims that aliens wish to check up on human activities, Shostak argues that extraterrestrials probably do not know that humans exist. And, he argues, even if they did, they would probably not care about earthly happenings. Shostak is a senior astronomer at the SETI (Search for Extraterrestrial Intelligence) Institute.

AS YOU READ, CONSIDER THE FOLLOWING QUESTIONS:
1. According to the author, what human activities do UFO supporters say aliens are interested in?

2. What is the one signal that Shostak says humans have sent to the stars?
3. At the end of his essay, the author writes that the idea that aliens have visited Earth is "self-indulgent." What do you think he means by this?

When it comes to alien activities, visiting Earth seems to be pretty high on the "to do" list. But does that make sense?

Three Possibilities

Approximately half the U.S. population suspects that extraterrestrials have come to our planet. This is such a controversial (and emotional) topic that its mere mention in one of these articles is usually sufficient to guarantee a storm of Web chat and high-voltage e-mails. In the end, of course, the matter of alien visitation will be decided by the evidence, not by the intensity of opinion. While I certainly expect that the Galaxy is home to many advanced societies, the quality of the evidence has so far failed to convince me that any of them have emissaries on our planet.

But let's back off to our neutral corners for a moment and consider an intimately related question: why would aliens be visiting now? According to the most popular view of this matter, extraterrestrial craft have been flitting across our skies since 1947. That's 55 years in a planetary history of 4,600,000,000 years. If we assume for the moment that these claims are real, this chronology tells us immediately that either (1) we are the beneficiaries of an enormously rare event (one chance in 100 million, or if you want to argue that no aliens would visit until they detected oxygen in our atmosphere, one chance in 40 million), (2) the aliens routinely visit Earth, or (3) our activities (nuclear

FAST FACT

Iain Murray of the Competitive Enterprise Institute states that only about 10 percent of stars with planets nearby are likely to have a planet that is hospitable to life.

In this illustration, the enormous spiral arms of our Milky Way galaxy hang in the sky over a bustling alien city located on a remote planet.

tests, environmental degradation, etc.) have attracted the aliens' attention, and encouraged them to drop by.

Highly Improbable

The first possibility, that we just happened to luck out (being around for the first and only alien encounter), is less probable than that you, not someone, but you will win next month's lottery jackpot. It strains credulity, to use polite vernacular.

The second possibility, that Earth hosts extraterrestrials on a routine basis, and therefore a visit during your lifetime is not particularly improbable, deserves a bit more scrutiny. The question is, how often do they visit? If it's only once in a few tens of millions of years, we're back to the first possibility, and the odds are highly stacked against you being one of the lucky visitees. But some folk claim that aliens have glissaded to Earth in historical times (five millennia ago, when the pyramids were built, or one millennium ago, when the Nazca Indians elected to decorate the Peruvian desert floor with glyphs of turkeys and other of their favorite fauna). If any of this is true, it argues for visits at least once every 1,000 years or so. The problem with this is that barring some reason for them to visit humans in particular (a possibility we consider below) it implies that there have been millions of expeditions to Earth! We may send the occasional anthropological research team to Borneo, but we don't send millions. And it's a lot easier to get to Borneo than to traverse hundreds or thousands of light-years. This, too, seems to be an unlikely explanation for visitors now.

Aliens Could Not Know About Us and Could Not Quickly Reach Us

Finally, we consider door number three—we have enticed the aliens with human activity. Let's set aside the question of whether advanced galactic societies would have the slightest interest in our wars, our pollution problems, or our reproductive systems. The real question is, how would they know about us at all?

In fact, there's only one clear and persistent "signal" that Homo sapiens has ever sent to the stars: our high-frequency radio transmissions, including television and radar. The Victorians (let alone the Egyptians or the Nazca Indians), despite all their technical sophistication, could never have been spotted from light-years away. Humans

Watterson. © 1989 by Universal Press Syndicate. Reproduced by permission.

This computer-generated image portrays a wormhole (upper right), a theoretical portal connecting distant points of the universe.

have been making their presence known to the universe only for the last 70 years or so.

And that's a problem. It means that even if, after receiving an earthly transmission, the aliens can immediately scramble their spacecraft and fly to Earth at the speed of light, they can't be farther than 8 light-years away to have arrived by 1947. There are four star systems within this distance. Count 'em, four. We're back to winning the lottery.

What about warp drive? Maybe the aliens can create wormholes and get here in essentially no time. It doesn't matter. Our signals travel at the speed of light, and this means that even with infinitely fast spacecraft, the aliens can't be farther off than 15 light-years to have reached our lovely planet by 1947. The number of star systems within 15 light-years is about three dozen. There would have to be 10 billion technically sophisticated societies in the Galaxy to have a reasonable chance of finding one camped out among the nearest three dozen stars. That's optimism of a high level indeed.

It's nice to think that either Earth or its human inhabitants have not only attracted the attention of galactic neighbors, but encouraged them to visit. But frankly, the numbers don't give much support to this somewhat self-indulgent idea.

EVALUATING THE AUTHOR'S ARGUMENTS:

This author uses statistics to argue that the chances of aliens visiting Earth are extremely slim. Do these statistics affect your opinion of his argument? If so, in what way? Explain your answer.

The Government Should Disclose the Existence of Aliens and UFOs

W. Richard Freeman

"The 'government' no longer will be able to conceal the presence of the [alien] visitors."

In the following viewpoint W. Richard Freeman contends that the government knows that extraterrestrials are visiting Earth but refuses to admit it. Although NASA has attempted to conceal documentation of UFOs, he maintains, retired astronauts admit that alien craft have been spotted during nearly every space mission. Once average citizens are able to enter space, Freeman asserts, it will become obvious to people that extraterrestrials do exist and do operate disc-like craft. As more facts emerge about UFOs, their operating methods, and their alien navigators, nations will have to share this information with each other rather than suppress it, Freeman predicts. This selection by Freeman, who resides in Wyoming, Minnesota, was published in *Fate Magazine,* which chronicles reports of UFOs, alien abductions, and other strange phenomena.

AS YOU READ, CONSIDER THE FOLLOWING QUESTIONS:
1. According to Freeman, how does NASA conceal the activities of aliens and their craft?
2. In the author's opinion, how must nations aid each other in the area of extraterrestrial contact?
3. Why does the author use quotes when he discusses the government?

A re there really UFOs? What are they? Where do they come from? These are only some of the questions being asked today by more people, as reports of sightings are distributed over the Internet.

This method of reporting and distributing the news of sightings is one of the factors that will ultimately pressure the "government" to reveal the truth of the visitors and their craft. Other factors that will influence the decision include a government-sponsored contest for private business to go into space, and the plans by business interests in Italy to build a hotel in space in the near future, when transportation costs come down and reliability figures of the craft go up.

Human Interaction with the Visitors

Burt Rutan, who designed the plane that flew non-stop around the Earth without refueling, also designed the rocket that won the first ten-million-dollar X-Prize in 2004. The contest is scheduled to become an annual event, as an incentive to speed private citizens into space.

The "government" no longer will be able to conceal the presence of the visitors when private citizens are able to witness the craft and perhaps interact with the visitors on a personal basis. The wish by some in the intelligence community to have all passengers to space hotels subject to an oath of secrecy is unrealistic and unworkable, another reason the truth will have to be disclosed soon.

Readers will notice I put the word "government" in quotes. This is because our constitutionally elected Congress, as a body, is purposely left out of the loop. Only certain members of Congress and

This crop circle that appeared in a Nebraska barley field in 1996 drew hundreds of visitors looking for evidence that the phenomenon was caused by a spaceship.

the Cabinet are apprised of some of the activities paid for by black budgets. Information about how many discs are "ours" (that is, constructed as a result of back-engineering) and how many are alien craft is so carefully guarded and compartmented on a need-to-know basis that only a select few know the details. A story that has followed this trail of secrecy says the information is carefully controlled by a non-elected body variously known as "MJ-12," "NSA Working Group," and other code names that have changed several times over the past 50 years.

Serious UFO Researchers

Those readers who still are not convinced of the presence of our non-human visitors should attend one of the national UFO conferences at the next opportunity. I was at the Denver MUFON [Mutual UFO Network] seminar that met in the middle of July 2004. It was the third conference I have attended [since February 2004], with each one more science-oriented than the previous one. A few years ago, I heard stories of attendees at UFO conferences running around the meeting hall wearing rubber alien masks, acting out some strange space drama. At the more recent conferences I have attended, I found none of that."

"THE AIR FORCE SAID TO FORGET IT . . . IT'S JUST OUR IMAGINATION."

Some people believe that astronauts, such as this one piloting a jet pack outside the space shuttle Challenger, *have encountered alien spacecraft during their missions.*

The atmosphere has been one of serious researchers and attendees attempting to answer very serious questions about reports of disc-like craft and their crews. Many other aspects of seemingly paranormal activity have been discussed, including remote viewing, crop circles, and Bigfoot sightings, as well as anti-gravity and modes of propulsion used in the discs.

A couple of the attendees I met were former "black budget" employees who worked on anti-gravity as long ago as 1970. Many ex-NASA employees also attend these conferences, and in some cases add their expertise to the discussions. One fact becomes clear very soon in the discussions: NASA is very active in concealing the activities of aliens and their craft. One also learns that the term "UFO" is not used at NASA—probably because they know full well what is following them in space. There are code words that change regularly for space crews to alert ground controllers to the presence of discs in the vicinity of our space probes, capsules, and the International Space Station. According to some retired astronauts and Russian cosmonauts, UFOs have been observed during virtually every space mission.

As more countries become members of the space-travel club, expect to receive more details of alien contact and interactions with ordinary humans. As Japan and China rapidly develop their space travel capability, sharing of information will become commonplace, as secrecy and compartmentalization give way to the necessity of nations aiding each other, whether for rescue or for mutual financial assistance and space education.

EVALUATING THE AUTHOR'S ARGUMENTS:

This author contends that the government has covered up evidence of UFOs. Do you agree with this assertion? Why or why not?

UFO Encounters Enrich Human Lives

Nick Redfern

"When we immerse ourselves in the world of the UFO, . . . wonderful life-changing experiences do follow."

Nick Redfern has authored several books and articles defending the existence of aliens and other paranormal phenomena. In the following viewpoint he argues that many people have undergone positive life changes following their run-in with alien spaceships. He focuses on the case of his friend, Tracie Austin-Peters. The author explains how Austin-Peters's UFO sighting altered the course of her life for the better. Following that incident, Austin-Peters appeared in a TV documentary about her encounter, hosted UFO conferences, and now hosts and produces a public access talk show on the paranormal. Experiences such as these cause Redfern to conclude that UFO encounters can lead to extraordinary life changes.

AS YOU READ, CONSIDER THE FOLLOWING QUESTIONS:
1. Describe the object that Tracie Austin-Peters reported seeing on May 14, 1996.

2. What were the responses of the woman and the man whom Austin-Peters approached in the parking lot, as relayed by the author?
3. What is the name of Austin-Peters's public access show?

I recently lectured for the Dallas–Fort Worth, Texas-based branch of the Mutual UFO Network (MUFON). After the lecture and as we ate dinner in a nearby restaurant, one of the people in attendance asked me if studies had been undertaken to determine the extent to which UFO encounters could be considered life-changing events. "That's a good question," I replied.

And it set me thinking: How many people's lives have taken radically different courses than they could previously—and possibly—have imagined, in the wake of some form of UFO encounter? My guess is a large number. And none more so than a good friend of mine, and a fellow-Brit, named Tracie Austin-Peters, who had her own encounter with a mysterious aerial object in 1996.

Spotting a UFO

Tracie was born in England in 1965, and having studied at Cauldon College of Further Education in 1984, relocated to London a year later to teach in various schools and study at the Guildhall School of Music & Drama, as a concert pianist.

It was during this period that Tracie first began to take an interest in the UFO mystery. In 1989, Tracie moved back to her hometown of Staffordshire and seven years later had a UFO sighting that went on to have a profound and life-changing effect on her.

"It was about 3 o'clock in the afternoon on May 14, 1996," states Tracie today, "and it was quite a clear and sunny day. I'd got about an hour and a half free before I had to be back at work, and decided that because it was so nice, I would drive up to the woods nearby with a book and read for a while.

"I headed for the local shop and pulled up on the car park, as I was going to get a few items to take with me. But as I got out of the car, I got an immediate urge to look up. It was just like something had told me to look up, although I didn't hear a voice. It was more like an impulse.

This simulation shows what it might be like to view a flying saucer through a car windshield in broad daylight.

"I knew directly where to look, too. And as I looked up, I saw a really unusually shaped object that looked like a boomerang or a V-shaped craft. It was silent, it was black, and as I stood watching it, I thought to myself: I need to get a grip on this. What am I looking at?"

The Witnesses

Tracie continues, "I'm quite a logical person, and I wondered at first if it was a large bird of some kind, but it wasn't. The wings were just stretched out and it wasn't moving like a bird. It was sort of turning anti-clockwise. And it certainly wasn't an airplane or a hang-glider. I knew I had to grab someone to see if they could see it, too.

"There was a woman near me getting her child out of her car and I said to her, 'Excuse me, I hope you don't think I'm being silly, but can you see what I can see in the sky?' She replied, 'You mean that black thing?' I said, 'Yes,' and we both stood and watched it. But I got a very strong feeling, like it was giving off a thought, saying: 'Have a good look at me because what you are seeing is real.'"

At that point, something truly strange occurred. "I watched it and then it did the most bizarre thing. It shrunk itself into a black sphere but continued to move anti-clockwise. But the strange thing was that the lady who was with me didn't see it change shape. I thought this was ridiculous, and ran across the car park to grab someone else. He saw it, too, but didn't know what it was. But as I watched, the object then transformed back to its original shape and then an appendage came out of the middle, which made it look like an arrowhead.

"It then headed off in what I thought was the direction of the woods. So, I jumped in the car and headed off there, too. I scanned the sky but didn't see it again, unfortunately. Well, I was due to start work again about 4:30 p.m., so I went home and telephoned Irene Bott of the Staffordshire UFO Group and told her what had happened. Irene told me to write it all down and draw a picture of the object—which I did. I also phoned a local UFO group in my area, too, and they said they would look into it.

"Suddenly, at that point, I got this feeling again to look up in the sky and was amazed to see this same object flying directly over my house. It was so strange; I wasn't frightened—just surprised and excited. And the whole thing took on such a magical atmosphere. And again, I got the feeling that the object wanted to be seen. I'm not too brilliant at heights, but it was much lower than your average aircraft. Again, it was moving in an anti-clockwise way and I watched it until it vanished."

The story was not quite over, however. "Three days later, the UFO group phoned me back to say that they had had a call from a guy who didn't want to leave his name but who lived about four miles from me. They told me that he said he'd seen three black boomerang-shaped objects flying over his house, and I just couldn't believe it."

To this day, Tracie says, the extraordinary events of May 14, 1996 remain firmly fixed in her mind and she is certain that something truly out-of-this-world took place.

FAST FACT

Anthropologist Krista Henriksen says her study of alleged alien abductees suggests that the experience can be pleasant. Henriksen told the *Edmonton News* in 2002 that the aliens "tell people they're not alone, that they're special, they're chosen for a purpose."

Amazing Life Changes

Shortly after Tracie's encounter, the British television channel BBC Digital was made aware of her sighting, and during the making of a TV documentary, "Over the Moon," Tracie told her story and re-enacted her sighting. Galvanized by this, in June of 1996 she hosted her first UFO conference, which became a major success. Radio appearances followed, as did articles in local newspapers and invitations to speak on the subject at various organizations. A second conference followed in 1998. But it was in 1999 that Tracie's life changed radically. It was that year, after we traveled together to the annual LAPIS UFO conference in northern England, that Tracie met UFO and "rods" researcher Jim Peters, who was delivering a presentation at the conference with Jose Escamilla. Romance quickly blossomed and two years later Jim and Tracie were married and living just outside of Los Angeles.

Today, Tracie is both the host and producer of her own public access talk show based in Santa Clarita, California, titled "Let's Talk . . . Paranormal," that regularly discusses a whole range of UFO-related top-

"HOWDY STRANGER!"

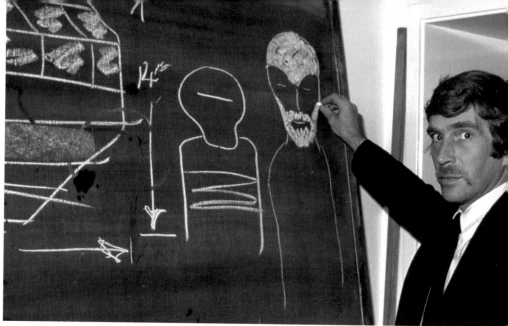

A former policeman who claims to have been abducted by aliens details his experience at a UFO seminar in Manchester, England, in 1982.

ics and airs in the region on Monday evenings on Channel 20 at 10 P.M. She recently became a finalist in the 24th Annual Telly Awards and is now networking her show as far afield as Tucson, Arizona, where her show airs every Wednesday afternoon at 2 P.M. on Channel 73, and is currently arranging for her show to be aired nationally.

Would Tracie now be living in sunny California with her own TV show if it wasn't for that chance encounter? Who knows? But her experiences do serve to amply demonstrate that when we immerse ourselves in the world of the UFO, both weird and wonderful life-changing experiences do follow.

EVALUATING THE AUTHOR'S ARGUMENTS:

This author uses one detailed example in support of his claim that people who spot UFOs often undergo amazing life changes. How effective is this method, in your opinion? Explain.

Viewpoint 4

Humanity Could Be Advanced by Alien Contact

H. Paul Shuch

"If we're incredibly fortunate, [aliens'] transmissions might contain their own social and cultural history."

The discovery of alien life could benefit humankind, proposes H. Paul Shuch in this viewpoint. The races we could come upon range from extremely sophisticated to slightly more developed than our own, he contends. He writes that humanity would learn the most from a civilization just slightly more advanced than ours. In that case, he suggests, the extraterrestrials may teach humans how to survive through cooperation rather than war. Additionally, aliens could teach us to use Earth's resources while preserving its environment, Shuch writes. H. Paul Shuch is executive director of SETI, which searches space for evidence of extraterrestrial intelligence.

AS YOU READ, CONSIDER THE FOLLOWING QUESTIONS:

1. Who is Frank Drake?

H. Paul Shuch, "The Search for Extraterrestrial Intelligence: The 40-Year Search for Extraterrestrial Intelligence Continues to Evolve. What Will the Next 40 Years Bring?" *The Futurist,* May/June 2003, pp. 52–55. Copyright © 2003 by the World Future Society. Reproduced by permission.

2. What would happen if humans stumbled upon a race a billion years older than humankind, in the author's opinion?
3. What does the author believe should be the focus of SETI?

We were the only game in town—the sole sentient species in the cosmos. Or so the mainstream scientific community thought in 1959. That perception wouldn't hold for long, however. Less than half a century later, scientific evidence would suggest that our civilization could be but one among many.

In 1959, young radio astronomer Frank Drake was fresh out of graduate school when he hit upon a seemingly ludicrous idea. Why not use his employer's radio telescope to search for intelligently generated signals from the stars? He cautioned himself to do so quietly; this science-fiction search might well be professional suicide. So he set to work, quietly assembling a crude, one-channel listening station to train on two nearby, sunlike stars.

Then, the 1959 Cocconi and Morrison article came out. In a brief paper in the scientific journal *Nature,* two Cornell professors, Giuseppe

SETI Institute president Frank Drake explains his Drake Equation, which he formulated to estimate the number of civilizations in the Milky Way galaxy.

The Drake Equation

In 1961, astronomer Frank Drake developed a mathematical equation to determine how many intelligent alien civilizations might be present in our galaxy. Each step in the equation represents a likely factor connected to the existence of a civilization.

$$R \times F_p \times n_e \times f_1 \times$$

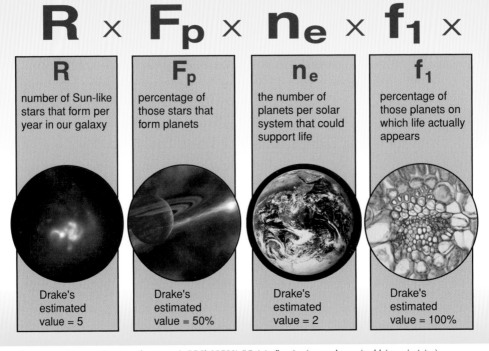

R	F_p	n_e	f_1
number of Sun-like stars that form per year in our galaxy	percentage of those stars that form planets	the number of planets per solar system that could support life	percentage of those planets on which life actually appears
Drake's estimated value = 5	Drake's estimated value = 50%	Drake's estimated value = 2	Drake's estimated value = 100%

Source: SETI League (www.setileague.org); PBS's NOVA "Origins" series (www.pbs.org/wgbh/nova/origins).

Cocconi and Philip Morrison, proposed the very search that Drake was setting out to perform. This is a prime example of what I call the Parenthood Principle: When a great idea is ready to be born, it goes out in search of a parent. Sometimes, it finds more than one. Now . . . Drake had to go public. But discretion still ruled the day. Even his first detection, of a classified military aircraft, was of necessity held close to the chest.

Redefining SETI

Today, the search for extraterrestrial intelligence (SETI) has emerged out of the fringes into the scientific mainstream. In 40 years, researchers have developed technologies the likes of which young Drake could scarcely have dreamed. As Drake grayed into the elder statesman of an established scientific discipline, thousands of people have conducted hundreds of searches for our cosmic compan-

Scientists have evidence to make better guesses on some of the factors than on others. If one factor in the equation changes, the outcome will change accordingly. Since 1961, other scientists have used or modified this basic equation, which has since become known as the Drake equation.

$$\mathbf{f_i} \times \mathbf{f_c} \times \mathbf{L} = \mathbf{N}$$

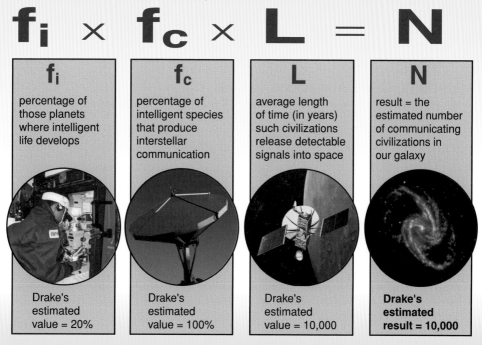

$\mathbf{f_i}$	$\mathbf{f_c}$	$\mathbf{L}$	$\mathbf{N}$
percentage of those planets where intelligent life develops	percentage of intelligent species that produce interstellar communication	average length of time (in years) such civilizations release detectable signals into space	result = the estimated number of communicating civilizations in our galaxy
Drake's estimated value = 20%	Drake's estimated value = 100%	Drake's estimated value = 10,000	**Drake's estimated result = 10,000**

ions, scanning billions of microwave and optical channels and spending millions of dollars in the process. SETI is no longer a four-letter word. But for all of that effort, we are today no more successful in detecting extraterrestrial intelligence than Drake was with his first search. . . .

We can improve our chances for success by redefining SETI. At present, SETI is as narrowly focused as the spectral emissions that we hope to intercept. What began as a search for microwave beacons should be expanded to encompass all signaling technologies, whether or not we have achieved them yet at our present level of societal and technical adolescence.

Might we someday launch robotic interstellar probes? If so, then we should have an organized strategy for seeking out such probes launched by more-advanced societies. Can we imagine the day when we will be capable of great feats of estroengineering? Then our present efforts should include a search for the engineering marvels of our more-capable neighbors. Might our own starships someday leave a detectable residue? Then the search for the advanced propulsion signatures of others should be on our agenda. If we can imagine it, then we should be looking for it. As Haldane's Law teaches us, the universe is not only queerer than we imagine; it is queerer than we can imagine.

Encountering Advanced Races

A common myth holds that our brothers and sisters in space will hand us a silver platter loaded with solutions to all of humankind's problems: cures for disease and poverty and ignorance and prejudice, which everyone knows are trivial matters for those advanced beings conquering the interstellar gulf.

Everyone is most likely wrong. Since ours is a relatively young planet orbiting a fairly new star, it's a cinch to speculate that we're the newcomers on the block. Top astrophysicists have estimated that other civilizations could well be anywhere from a thousand to a billion years older than our own. If the first extraterrestrial civilization we encounter is at the upper end of that age continuum, SETI scientists will be

This infrared image shows a galaxy located 12 million light-years from Earth. Some scientists believe the sheer remoteness of neighboring galaxies makes extraterrestrial visits unlikely.

lucky to even recognize its artifacts as manifestations of intelligence, let alone interpret them. Such an ancient race would be as far ahead of us as we are beyond bacteria.

We will be far better served if our cosmic communicators have advanced only a little bit beyond us. If they lead us by, let us say, a million years, then they might make their culture known to us much as we communicate with household pets. This is speculative to be sure, but what if they regard us much as we regard dogs? What do we stand to gain? And to lose?

One could argue that *Canis familiaris* (domestic dog) enjoys a longer life span and better nutrition than his wild ancestor; that by taking him under our protection, humans have given him a higher standard of living. Pulling our sleds, herding our sheep, guarding our children, and leading our blind are small prices for him to pay for the benefits we benevolently bestow. But did anyone ever bother to ask Fido how he feels about the arrangement?

We Have Everything to Gain

Science fiction is full of cautionary tales of humanity being subdued and subjugated by advanced aliens. Surely if their technology is capable of announcing its presence across the cosmic gulf, they have the capacity to come here in conquest. Better to let well enough alone, some argue.

But wait—SETI is all about communication, not contact. Unless we've got the laws of nature all wrong, beings of an advanced civilization at the far end of the galaxy will still take 50,000 to 70,000 years to get here, assuming they want to know about us. That distant cousin of yours in Kansas receiving your Christmas card might just take your casual "drop by sometime" seriously and show up on your doorstep next Thanksgiving, but extraterrestrial beings? Not likely.

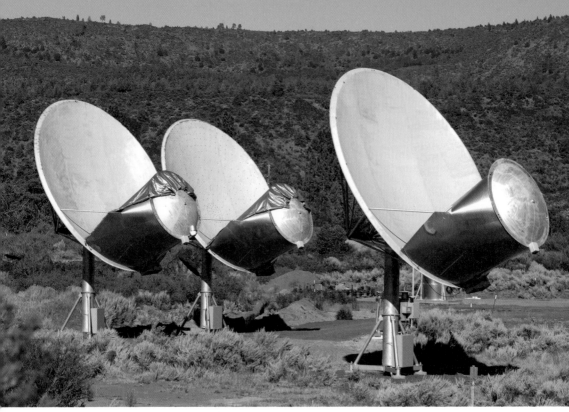

These radio telescope antennas located in California are part of a SETI research facility searching for signals of intelligent extraterrestrial life.

For one thing, they haven't been invited. We inhabit a paranoid planet. Pressures from governing bodies and private citizens alike have prompted most scientific organizations and SETI research facilities to adopt a policy that prohibits interstellar transmission lest we give ourselves away. With only a few minor exceptions, we have refrained from shouting in the jungle. The act of listening in no way reveals our position or our interest; it makes us no more vulnerable to invasion and domination than we would be by turning a deaf ear to the universe. Given that SETI is a passive activity, it would seem we have nothing to lose in listening.

And everything to gain.

The Best Scenario
I've skipped over that other alternative: that we could well encounter a civilization just a little bit more advanced than ours—one that . . . has learned, in generations not too remote, to harness its planet's resources in an environmentally responsible way, to embrace genetic engineering

with compassion and reason, to ensure the survival of its species through cooperation rather than conflict. These are lessons we need to learn if we are to survive the next thousand years or so and thus to reach their level. If we're incredibly fortunate, their transmissions might contain their own social and cultural history, including a glimpse into their crossroads and crises. But even lacking such details, a signal received from such a society will testify to life's capacity for survival against long odds. We would do well to learn from their example.

Part of that example is in the medium itself. If beings from a modestly advanced civilization choose to fling photons our way, then we can conclude that they have deemed it safe to do so. Here, too, we might do well to learn from their example by abandoning our planetary paranoia and beginning to transmit warm greetings to other young civilizations near our point on the developmental continuum. Should the phone happen to ring, etiquette demands we answer it pleasantly.

EVALUATING THE AUTHOR'S ARGUMENTS:

What point is the author making by comparing the domestic dog to humankind? Does this comparison work, in your opinion? Why or why not?

Glossary

abductee: Someone who claims to have been abducted by aliens.

debunker: A skeptic who seeks to disprove claims of UFO sightings.

extraterrestrial (ET): Originating from outside of Earth.

galaxy: A collection of stars held together by their combined gravities. Our galaxy is the Milky Way.

hypnagogic hallucinations: Visions that a person may have while falling asleep.

hypnopompic hallucinations: Visions that a person may experience upon waking.

IFO (identified flying object): A UFO that is determined to have an earthly cause.

light-year: The distance that light travels in a year, or about 6 trillion miles.

meteor: A solid particle that enters Earth's atmosphere from space.

NASA (National Aeronautics and Space Administration): The U.S. government agency in charge of learning about and exploring the universe.

Project Blue Book: The U.S. Air Force's investigation of flying saucers which lasted from 1947 to 1969.

SETI (Search for Extraterrestrial Intelligence): A program that seeks out signals from alien civilizations.

UFO (unidentified flying object): An object in the sky whose identity cannot be explained; also called a flying saucer.

UFOlogist: One who studies UFO sightings and attempts to identify their origin.

universe: All of the space and matter that exists.

Thinking Critically About UFOs

Are UFOs really alien spacecraft? Or do witnesses mistake normal things—natural phenomena or man-made objects, for example—for flying saucers? As the arguments in this book indicate, significant numbers of people emphatically answer yes to both of these questions. Nearly every claim about UFOs, it seems, triggers both strong support and strong opposition, and people on all sides of the issue back up their claims with what they consider persuasive evidence.

But in fact, little hard evidence exists on the subject of UFOs. Although investigators and eyewitnesses have reported UFO sightings, encounters, and abductions in detail, no definitive physical proof of aliens or their spacecraft exists. Skeptics insist that without scientific proof, claims of alien spaceship sightings are not credible. UFO believers, on the other hand, insist that UFO sightings are unexpected, sudden, and often fleeting, which naturally explains the lack of documentation and scientific evidence. Besides, UFO supporters ask, where is the proof that alien spaceships do *not* exist?

Deciding what to believe requires careful evaluation of competing claims based on hypothetical reasoning. This reasoning process requires you to think critically about a claim—what it means and how and by whom it is presented. It also requires you to scrutinize the evidence offered in defense of the claim. In this way you can determine which arguments are based on solid facts and objective analysis and which are based on unreliable assumptions and personal opinions.

Examining a Hypothesis

To analyze claims presented in a written article, a reader must first identify the author's hypothesis. Most authors form a hypothesis—a clear, specific, and theoretically provable statement—that expresses the main point of the article in one or two sentences. The hypothesis is the crux of the article. Without identifying it, readers may not be able to figure out what the author is trying to prove or disprove and are less likely to be persuaded to agree with the author's point of view.

Each contributor to this anthology makes a different claim about UFOs that can be summarized in a succinct hypothesis. Here are three examples:

Author	Hypothesis
Paul Devereux	Natural earth lights are sometimes mistakenly perceived as alien spaceships or other paranormal phenomena.
Dennis Balthaser	Physical evidence and historical documentation prove that UFOs are extraterrestrial spacecraft.
Joe Nickell	People who claim to have been abducted by aliens are delusional or fantasy prone.

Practice identifying and concisely expressing the hypotheses made by the other authors in this book.

Gathering the Evidence

After stating a hypothesis, an author then presents evidence intending to prove it, to build a case convincing enough to persuade readers to agree with his or her conclusions and change their own minds. As a reader, you must identify and analyze the evidence to decide two things: Is the evidence credible? and Does the evidence prove the hypothesis? While many different kinds of evidence can be presented to test a hypothesis, some are more commonly used in arguments about ETs and UFOs. These include eyewitness testimony; expert opinion; research and poll results; physical evidence that can be held or measured; and statements of fact, or assertions that are presented as true.

The first step is to collect the evidence presented by an author. A list of evidence used in Dennis Balthaser's article, for example, will look something like this:

1. It has not been possible to produce some physical proof of alien spacecraft because the government is withholding it.
2. In at least five cases, there is physical proof of mysterious encounters with unidentified craft.
3. Many UFO witnesses are distinguished, respectable, and even important military or government officials.

4. Proof that UFOs existed even in ancient times is found in the Bible and in medieval artwork.
5. Thousands of people have captured images of UFOs on videotape or film and in photographs. This evidence has been authenticated by experts.
6. The government holds authenticated documents that reveal that the air force has investigated and still is secretly investigating UFO sightings.
7. Alleged alien abductees have unexplainable marks on their bodies, have implants in their bodies, or have experienced time lapses in their lives.
8. Radar has detected unidentifiable objects in areas of the sky where no aircraft were reported at the time.
9. Military aircraft have been unable to catch up to mysterious flying objects or have seen them disappear.
10. Several researchers and writers distort the facts about UFOs to promote their own views that UFOs are not alien ships.
11. One researcher reports that there are more than five thousand cases on file in which physical evidence of UFOs was found.

Analyzing the Evidence

After gathering an author's evidence, the next step is to evaluate its credibility. No matter how authoritative or convincing a supporting statement may sound at first, look more closely. Certain kinds of supporting material may be more convincing or more provable than others. Ultimately, the evidence that is most convincing will show you, not simply tell you, that the author's hypothesis is valid. Unverified statements and uninformed opinions, for example, are generally considered weak, unreliable evidence because they do not *demonstrate* that a claim is true.

In discussing paranormal topics, for which hard proof may be hard to produce, authors often use personal experience and witness testimony as evidence. However, such first-person accounts are usually uncorroborated and can be undependable and colored by personal bias. Witnesses have a tendency to forget some details, exaggerate others, and remember some incorrectly. In addition, some witnesses may have ulterior motives, such as a desire for fame. The best testimony, therefore, comes from a reliable source—someone with a proven record of study or experience in the field, for instance—and is repeated, or verified, by several other unrelated witnesses.

Likewise, critically consider all other kinds of evidence offered as proof before you accept it. For example, research and poll results are commonly used to support the existence of alien spacecraft. This statistical data can be persuasive evidence if it is collected in studies that follow the scientific method and are conducted by respectable researchers. Similarly, physical evidence can be convincing if it is legitimate and not tampered with or doctored. Expert opinion can serve as good support for an argument but might be challenged since even authorities in the same field disagree about the true nature of UFOs. You should examine the expert's credentials and character to determine whether the person is a reliable source. Be especially aware of statements presented as fact. Information that is presented as true should still be verifiable and not simply based on an author's opinion.

An example from the text can show you how to apply these critical thinking tools. Examine the second piece of evidence presented by Balthaser: In at least five cases, there is physical proof of mysterious encounters with unidentified craft. Physical evidence of any phenomenon is often seen as compelling. However, you must consider what that evidence is before you can conclude that it is legitimate. The author points out that the government and the military investigated the alleged encounter sites, debris left behind, and an audio recording of one of the alleged incidents. But he does not relate the details of each investigation: Is it reasonable to conclude that an alien encounter must have occurred simply because government and military officials investigated a mysterious incident? Does the fact that the government did not discredit or offer an alternative explanation for the evidence it analyzed mean the evidence is therefore proof of a flying saucer?

The evidence Balthaser presents—imprints in the soil and burnt vegetation near UFO sites, for example—certainly seems to be proof of an aircraft landing. Yet the author does not discuss possible alternative explanations for these phenomena, such as the crash of a man-made airship. Here, the author seems to make a leap of logic by assuming that the craft must have been alien in nature. Author Steve Douglass, in contrast, might theorize that the evidence suggests a military craft landed there. Similarly, he might argue that the authenticated videotapes and photographs of

UFOs Balthaser presents as his fifth piece of evidence do not necessarily prove that the unidentified images were *alien* ships. While Balthaser does concede that some of these alleged UFO incidents were hoaxes or were explainable, he does not inform the reader of his criteria for determining which cases involved alien spacecraft and which did not.

It is up to you to decide whether the material Balthaser presents as proof is valid and reliable and if it adequately supports his hypothesis. For each piece of evidence offered by Balthaser, identify what kind of evidence it is and then assess its credibility. If you conclude that it is credible but it does not seem to logically support the author's hypothesis, note that as well.

Drawing a Conclusion

After you have evaluated all of Balthaser's evidence, make a conclusion about his hypothesis. Do you think he adequately supports his claim that UFOs are alien craft? Keep in mind that some types of evidence are more persuasive than others and some of the author's arguments may be stronger than others. You may place more confidence in solid facts or corroborated testimony and give less credence to uninformed opinion, for instance. Here is a template that you can use when evaluating an argument:

Author's name:

Author's hypothesis:

List of evidence:

Evaluation of the evidence, including what type of evidence it is, whether it appears to be valid, and whether it supports the author's hypothesis:

Draw a conclusion about whether the author has proved the hypothesis, and explain your answer in terms of the evidence that is most or least convincing:

Applying Hypothetical Reasoning to Paul Devereux's Article

Next, use hypothetical reasoning to critique Paul Devereux's viewpoint. His hypothesis is that natural earth lights are sometimes mistakenly perceived as alien spaceships or other paranormal phenomena.

The evidence he presents to support his assertion is:

1. The great majority of UFO sightings result from human misperception of man-made or heavenly objects, are illusions or hoaxes, or are reported by people who may be in an altered mental state or a trance.
2. The remainder of UFO reports may be caused by an exotic natural phenomenon called earth lights that scientists do not yet understand.
3. Earth lights sometimes have great longevity.
4. Earth lights seem to be associated with stresses in the earth's crust or other geological and meteorological sources of energy.
5. It is possible that there are alien civilizations throughout the universe but none of them has visited Earth.
6. Mysterious earth lights have been observed and explained in many different cultures throughout time.
7. Recent scientific discoveries of previously unknown phenomena suggest that it is possible for earth lights to have existed without having been studied or explained scientifically until now.
8. Witnesses who come near earth lights report having hallucinations, perhaps due to magnetic fields that affect the brain.
9. Earth lights seem to be a form of plasma that, according to witness reports, sometimes behaves as if it has a rudimentary intelligence. Recently scientists created plasmas in a laboratory that also behaved just like living cells.
10. The illogical effects that witnesses report may occur because earth lights theoretically exist only at the subatomic level but are somehow manifesting themselves on a larger scale. Laboratory studies have shown that other phenomena can be manifested in this way.

Now examine Devereux's evidence. Because the existence of earth lights is a theory, as yet unproven, much of this article is based on Devereux's own expert opinion, sometimes backed by scientific research findings. Expert opinion, however, is not in itself always reliable. This particular author is a researcher of unusual geophysical phenomena who has written several books on the subject, which you may decide lends credence to his opinions regarding the existence of earth lights.

For some of his evidence, the author relies on witness testimony, which can be undependable. The characteristics of earth lights described in points 8, 9, and 10, for example, are based on witnesses' reports. Devereux assumes that the witnesses are telling the truth about the mysterious phenomena they observed, but does not accept that the phenomena are caused by alien spaceships. Instead, Devereux cites scientific findings as an alternative explanation. In points 9 and 10, after he introduces reported properties of earth lights, he notes laboratory research that has reproduced those strange characteristics in controlled experiments. In this way he attempts to prove that earth lights exude natural, scientifically explained characteristics that credible witnesses have simply misinterpreted.

A critical reader may decide, however, that Devereux does not reveal enough information about the research he cites to judge whether it is sound on that basis alone. Perhaps more information will make this evidence more convincing: He notes that the plasma study was very recent and was conducted by scientists in Romania, so it may be possible to look up the study and evaluate it in more detail. Or, if you have determined from Devereux's credentials that his research sources can be trusted, then you might assume that the studies are credible.

Often Devereux depends on the reader to draw conclusions from his evidence. In support of point 6, for example, he examines different cultures' legends about mysterious earth lights to demonstrate that the phenomenon has existed throughout time and has been explained in many different ways. Presumably, he expects the reader to conclude that alien spaceships, too, are just another explanation that modern humans produce for an occurrence they still do not understand. However, Devereux does not explicitly state this. As you examine his piece, consider whether his arguments would have been stronger had he overtly drawn these conclusions for the reader.

After you have deliberated the evidence presented by Devereux, draw a conclusion about whether he has convincingly proved his hypothesis. Cite the most persuasive and least persuasive evidence in your explanation, in the same way that you evaluated Balthaser's article.

Balancing the Evidence

Weighing the evidence for and against UFOs can be a tricky process. You may need to analyze several articles on both sides of the issue before you have a good sense of the main points of contention in this debate. Once you have done so, you can balance the evidence on one side against that of the opposing side. Only then can you make a truly informed decision about whether alien visits to Earth are fact or fiction.

Organizations to Contact

Citizens Against UFO Secrecy, Inc. (CAUS)
Peter Gersten, PO Box 2443, Sedona, AZ 86339
(520) 203-0567
e-mail: caus@caus.org • ufolawyer@caus.org
Web site: www.caus.org

CAUS is a nonprofit public interest group that believes that extraterrestrials are in contact with Earth and that there is a campaign of secrecy to conceal this knowledge.

Committee for the Scientific Investigation of Claims of the Paranormal (CSICOP)
PO Box 703, Amherst, NY 14226
(716) 636-1425
e-mail: info@csicop.org
Web site: www.csicop.org

Established in 1976, the committee is a nonprofit organization that encourages the critical investigation of paranormal and fringe-science claims from a scientific point of view. It disseminates the results of such inquiries to the scientific community and the public.

Federal Bureau of Investigation (FBI)
J. Edgar Hoover Building, 935 Pennsylvania Ave. NW
Washington, DC 20535-0001
(202) 324-3000
Web site: http://foia.fbi.gov/room.htm

The Federal Bureau of Investigation is committed to important national security and law enforcement responsibilities. The FBI's electronic reading room offers published FBI findings and articles on UFOs, with such topics as "Animal/Cattle Mutilation" and "Roswell."

HBCC UFO Research
Box 1091, Houston, BC, Canada V0J-1Z0
(866) 262-1989

e-mail: hbccufo@hbccufo.com
Web site: www.hbccufo.com

This organization serves the Canadian UFO research community by covering sightings in Canada and other parts of the world. It categorizes flying saucer reports, archives news stories, and provides links to editorials and interviews pertaining to the UFO phenomenon.

J. Allen Hynek Center for UFO Studies (CUFOS)
2457 W. Peterson Ave., Chicago, IL 60659
(773) 271-3611
e-mail: infocenter@cufos.org
Web site: www.cufos.org

The aim of CUFOS, a nonprofit scientific organization, is to continually analyze the UFO phenomenon. The center acts as a clearinghouse for the reporting and researching of UFO experiences.

Mutual UFO Network
PO Box 369, Morrison, CO 80465-0369
(303) 932-7709
e-mail: webmaster@mufon.com
Web site: www.mufon.com

MUFON is dedicated to the scientific study of UFOs. It does so through cataloging and investigating UFO sightings, researching the UFO phenomenon, and educating people about UFOs. People can report UFO sightings by filling out a short form on its Web site.

National UFO Reporting Center
PO Box 45623, University Station, Seattle, WA 98145
(206) 722-3000
e-mail: director@ufocenter.com
Web site: www.nuforc.org

Founded in 1974, the center serves as a headquarters for reporting possible UFO sightings. Such reports are recorded and disseminated for objective research and information purposes.

Research Institute on Anomalous Phenomena
Robert W. Gray, 92 Cypress St., Rochester, NY 14620

e-mail: riap777@softhome.net

Web site: www.geocities.com/riap777/index.html

RIAP is an independent scientific-research body, established in Kharkiv (Ukraine) in 1992. It unites specialists and amateurs from many countries who seek to solve world mysteries.

SETI Institute
515 N. Whisman Rd., Mountain View, CA 94043
(650) 961-6633
Web site: www.seti.org

The SETI Institute is a private, nonprofit organization dedicated to scientific research, education, and public outreach on topics pertaining to the origin, nature, and prevalence of life in the universe. Its Center for SETI Research develops technology to search for signals from advanced technological civilizations in our galaxy.

Skeptics Society
PO Box 338, Altadena, CA 91001
(818) 794-3119
e-mail: skepticmag@aol.com
Web site: www.skeptic.com

The society is composed of scholars, scientists, and historians who promote the use of scientific methods to scrutinize nonscientific beliefs such as religion, superstition, mysticism, and New Age beliefs. It is devoted to the investigation of extraordinary claims and to the promotion of science and critical thinking.

Society for Scientific Exploration (SSE)
PO Box 3818, Charlottesville, VA 22903
e-mail: scientific_exploration@yahoo.com
Web site: www.scientificexploration.org

Affiliated with the University of Virginia's Department of Astronomy, the society seeks to provide a professional forum for presentations, criticisms, and debates concerning topics that it feels are ignored or given inadequate study by mainstream academia. Some of the questions it explores include whether there is credible evidence that extraterrestrial life exists in our galaxy and whether it has visited our solar system.

For Further Reading

Books

Bartholomew, Robert E., and George S. Howard, *UFOs and Alien Contact: Two Centuries of Mystery*. Amherst, NY: Prometheus Books, 1998. Two researchers make the case that most people who believe they have encountered or been abducted by UFOs actually have fantasy-prone personalities.

Birnes, William J., *The UFO Magazine UFO Encyclopedia: The Most Comprehensive Single-Volume UFO Reference in Print*. New York: Pocket Books, 2004. Exhaustive guide to UFOs, extraterrestrials, and abduction cases. Contains more than five thousand entries with photographs, diagrams, and commentary by UFOlogists.

Dolan, Richard M., *UFOs and the National Security State: Chronology of a Coverup, 1941–1973*. Rev. ed. Hampton Roads, VA: Hampton Roads, 2002. Documents UFO sightings from around the globe and reveals how government authorities have attempted to suppress reports of alien craft.

Herbst, Judith, *UFOs (The Unexplained)*. Minneapolis, MN: Lerner, 2004. An easy read that provides a very general overview of unidentified flying objects.

Hickman, Jim, *The Alien Menace*. Baltimore, MD: PublishAmerica, 2004. Provides evidence for flying saucers and claims that their inhabitants have taken hostile action against humans.

Hines, Terence, *Pseudoscience and the Paranormal*. 2nd ed. Amherst, NY: Prometheus Books, 2003. This author skeptically examines supernatural phenomena ranging from psychic abilities to UFO abductions.

Hopkins, Budd, *Witnessed: The True Story of the Brooklyn Bridge Abductions*. New York: Pocket Books, 1997. A noted UFO researcher details the bizarre series of events surrounding a famous alien abduction case.

Kitei, Lynne D., *The Phoenix Lights*. Hampton Roads, VA: Hampton Roads, 2004. A comprehensive exploration of the cause of the mile-long, V-shaped formation of lights seen by thousands of Arizonans in 1997.

Klass, Philip J., *The Real Roswell Crashed-Saucer Coverup.* Amherst, NY: Prometheus Books, 1997. Uses science and logic to debunk claims that the government concealed evidence of an alien spacecraft that crashed near Roswell, New Mexico, in 1947.

Leir, Roger K., *The Aliens and the Scalpel: Scientific Proof of Extraterrestrial Implants in Humans.* Columbus, NC: Granite, 1999. Details cases in which physical evidence of alien abduction and experimentation was found in abductees.

Mack, John E., *Passport to the Cosmos: Human Transformations and Alien Encounters.* New York: Crown, 1999. Written by a Harvard professor of psychiatry who believes in aliens, this book explores the significance of the abduction experience, with a focus on its cultural and psychological impact.

Mitton, Jacqueline, *Aliens.* Cambridge, MA: Candlewick, 1999. Maintains that intelligent life probably does not exist anywhere else in our solar system but may exist around other stars. Also explains the SETI project, which searches for signals from extraterrestrial civilizations.

Nardo, Don, *Extraterrestrial Life.* San Diego: Lucent Books, 2004. Offers a well-rounded analysis of the possibility of alien life and of the likelihood of UFOs visiting Earth.

Pauk, Walter, *Aliens and UFOs.* New York: Glencoe/McGraw-Hill, 2002. Part of the Critical Reading series, this book contains critical thinking questions that encourage students to thoughtfully consider the UFO phenomenon.

Redfern, Nick, *Body Snatchers in the Desert: The Horrible Truth at the Heart of the Roswell Story.* New York: Paraview Pocket Books, 2005. Redfern theorizes that the mysterious object that crashed near Roswell, New Mexico, was a balloon carrying people who had been used as guinea pigs to test the effects of radiation on humans.

Roberts, Andy, and Nick Redfern, *Strange Secrets: Real Government Files on the Unknown.* New York: Paraview Pocket Books, 2003. Two experienced writers on UFOs assert that governments habitually deny well documented cases of supernatural phenomena, including UFOs and extraterretrials.

Roleff, Tamara L., ed., *Alien Abductions.* San Diego: Greenhaven Press, 2003. Provides evidence in support of extraterrestrial abductions as well as alternate explanations for such experiences.

Shermer, Michael, *Why People Believe Weird Things: Pseudoscience, Superstition, and Other Confusions of Our Time.* 2nd ed. New York: Owl Books, 2002. Explains why pseudosciences and superstitions involving near-death experiences, alien abductions, witches, and cults, do not stand up to scientific rigor.

Stacy, Dennis W., Patrick Huyghe, and Harry Trumbore, *The Field Guide to UFOs: A Classification of Various Unidentified Aerial Phenomena Based on Eyewitness Accounts.* New York: Quill/HarperCollins, 2000. Identifies and categorizes dozens of different shapes of UFOs. Also describes extraordinary UFO encounters and provides skeptical explanations for some sightings.

Strieber, Whitley, *Confirmation: The Hard Evidence of Aliens Among Us.* New York: St. Martin's, 1999. Claims that amateur videotapes of UFOs, the massive amount of abduction testimony, and the implants that have been removed from close-encounter witnesses prove that ETs have visited Earth.

Periodicals, Reports, and Internet Sources

Balthaser, Dennis G., "My 10 Favorite UFO Cases," *Skywatcher,* February 2005. www.skywatch-international.org.

Berman, Bob, "Strange Universe," *Astronomy,* March 2001.

Blackmore, Susan, "Abduction by Aliens or Sleep Paralysis?" *Skeptical Inquirer,* May 1998.

Carroll, Robert Todd, "Alien Abductions," *Skeptic's Dictionary,* September 5, 2005. www.skepdic.com.

———, "UFOs (Unidentified Flying Objects)," *Skeptic's Dictionary,* July 15, 2005. www.skepdic.com.

Corrales, Scott, "Abductions: The Crucible of Nightmares," *Fate,* May 2000.

———, "There Were Humans Among Them," *Fate,* May 2003.

CQ Researcher, "The Search for Extraterrestrials," March 5, 2004.

Darling, David, "Earthlights," *Encyclopedia of Astrobiology, Astronomy, and Spaceflight.* www.daviddarling.info.

Dolan, Richard M., "Everywhere, by Stealth," *UFO Magazine,* October/November 2001.

Filer, George A., "Filer's Files #29-2001," Mutual UFO Network, July 15, 2001. http://ufoinfo.com/filer/2001/ff_0129.shtml.

Gleghorn, Michael, "UFOs and Alien Beings," Probe Ministries, 2003. www.probe.org.

Hall, Charles James, interviewed by Paola Harris, Colorado Springs, CO, July 2003. www.paolaharris.it/english.html.

Klass, Philip J., "A Field Guide to UFOs," *Astronomy,* September 1997.

Krauss, Lawrence M., "Odds Are Stacked When Science Tries to Debate Pseudoscience," *New York Times,* April 30, 2002.

McAndrew, James, *The Roswell Report: Case Closed.* Washington, DC: U.S. Government Printing Office, 1997.

McClelland, Susan, and John Betts, "UFOs . . . Seriously: Is There a Middle Ground Between Skepticism and Belief?" *Maclean's,* August 13, 2001.

Park, Robert L., "Welcome to Planet Earth," *Sciences,* May 2000.

Paynter, Royston, "Stupid UFOlogy Tricks," Internet UFO Skeptics, 2001. www.webfellows.com/tufop.

Perlman, David, "Search for Extraterrestrial Life Moves to the Forefront," *San Francisco Chronicle,* December 15, 2003.

Posner, Gary P., "ETs May Be *Out There* . . . but He Says They're *Not Here:* An Interview with Philip J. Klass, the World's Leading UFO Skeptic," *Skeptic,* 1999.

Rees, Martin, "Our Greatest Quest," *New Scientist,* July 12, 2003.

Richardson, Jim, and Allen Richardson, "Gonzo Science; Persinger and the Unified Theory of the Paranormal," *Ripsaw,* September 2004.

Sheaffer, Robert, "UFOs Hold and Cold," *Skeptical Inquirer,* September/October 2003.

Space 2001, "Astronaut Encounters," 2001. www.space-2001.net.

Taylor, Lynn, "A Pound of Flesh," Alien Abduction Experience and Research, June 30, 1998. www.abduct.com.

Twitchell, David E., "Is the Day of UFO Disclosure Near?" *Skywatcher,* June 2005. www.skywatch-international.org.

U.S. House of Representatives, 107th Cong., "Life in the Universe," Subcommittee of Space and Aeronautics, Committee on Science, July 11, 2001. www.house.gov/science/hearings/index.htm.

Viggiani, Victor, "Disclosure: The Ultimate Terrestrial Imperative," International MetaPhysical and Scientific Symposium, Brisbane, Australia, August 2003.

Wilson, Jim, "When UFOs Arrive: The U.S. and Other World Governments Already Have Detailed Secret Plans for First Contact," *Popular Mechanics,* February 2004.

Web Sites

UFO Info (www.ufoinfo.com). This site offers coverage on a wide array of UFO topics, including news reports on UFOs and space exploration, listings of UFO sightings, and a weekly update of stories compiled by Mutual UFO Network Eastern director George Filer. It also provides contact information for various magazines on paranormal phenomena as well as forums where people can discuss subjects like UFOs and aliens.

UFO Skeptic (www.ufoskeptic.org). An information site on the UFO phenomenon by and for professional scientists. Contains links to reports, scientific studies, and journals that examine the likelihood of aliens visiting Earth and offer alternate explanations for UFOs.

Index

Picture Credits

Cover: © Victor Habbick Visions/Photo Researchers, Inc.
AP/Wide World Photos, 25, 46, 88
© Julian Baum/Photo Researchers, Inc., 45, 94
© Bettmann/CORBIS, 12 (inset), 40, 63 (inset)
© Paul Chinn/*San Francisco Chronicle*/CORBIS, 22
Columbia Pictures/Photofest, 66
© CORBIS, 69
© Christian Darkin/Photo Researchers, Inc., 26, 28, 59
© Phil Dauber/Photo Researchers, Inc., 39
© David A. Hardy, *Futures: 50 Years in Space*/Photo Researchers, Inc., 82
© David Hardy/Photo Researchers, Inc., 12
© Roger Harris/Photo Researchers, Inc., 84
© Magrath/Folsom/Photo Researchers, Inc., 32
Mary Evans Picture Library, 19 (both), 42 (both), 52, 63
Mary Evans Picture Library/Michael Buhler, 53, 77
NASA Headquarters – Greatest Images of NASA (NASA-HQ-GRIN), 90
NASA Jet Propulsion Laboratory (NASA-JPL), 102
© Pekka Parviainen/Photo Researchers, Inc., 35, 48
© Roger Ressmeyer/CORBIS, 14
© Royalty-Free/CORBIS, 50
© Dr. Seth Shostak/Photo Researchers, Inc., 99, 104
© Topham/The Image Works, 97
© Victor Habbick Visions/Photo Researchers, Inc., 16, 74, 79
Scott Weiss, 13, 21, 33, 75, 100–101

About the Editor

Jamuna Carroll is an editor, a poet, a promotions writer, and a former columnist. After receiving her bachelor's degree in writing and mass communication from Arizona State University, she relocated to San Diego. There, she writes, promotes events, attends concerts, and volunteers for Meals on Wheels. *Opposing Viewpoints: Marijuana* and *At Issue: Do Children Have Rights?* are among the anthologies she has compiled.